DANCING WITH THE BEAR

THE BEAR

A Serial Entrepreneur Goes East

DANCING WITH THE BEAR

A Serial Entrepreneur
Goes East

Roger Shashoua

GMB

GMB Publishing Ltd.
23–24 Smithfield Street
London EC1A 9LF
United Kingdom

525 South 4th Street, #241
Philadelphia, PA 19147
United States of America

www.globalmarketbriefings.com

This edition first published 2007 by GMB Publishing Ltd. All rights reserved.

© Roger Shashoua Hardcopy ISBN 978-1-84673-076-4
E-book ISBN 978-1-84673-077-1

British Library Cataloguing in Publication Data

A CIP record for this book is available from the British Library

---

Library of Congress Cataloguing-in Publication Data

Typeset by Saxon Graphics Ltd., Derby
Printed and bound in Great Britain By
Cambridge University Press

Contents

Acknowledgements

Jonathan Reuvid is an author and editor of business books, with more than 30 titles to his name. He is Senior Editor at GMB Publishing and Senior Consultant Editor to the business and reference division of Kogan Page. Formerly Director of European Operations for a US Fortune 500 company, he has been engaged in joint venture development in China for more than 20 years.

Acknowledgements

There are many friends and family to thank for their contributions to the writing and publication of this book. First, the companions in my adventures – in particular my brother Roddy and my elder son Mark, whose recollections of events are as vivid and sometimes clearer than my own – have set me right on some of the factual detail while reading the early drafts. Thanks also to my sister Joyce and her husband Angus James who have patiently read successive drafts and offered constructive criticism and to my younger son Daniel. I am especially grateful to my friend and travel companion Nicholas Berry for his advice and the Foreword, which neatly pinpoints the problem facing all serial entrepreneurs – what to do next.

And so to the publishing professionals. I am grateful to my daughter Deanne for her close involvement throughout the writing and editing process and to my publisher Peter Chadwick for taking on the publication of a text that is not in the business book mainstream. Last, but not least, my appreciation goes to Jonathan Reuvid, my literary adviser, for his continuing input from inception of the book to publication.

Roger Shashoua

Foreword

THE HARE AND THE TORTOISE

What happens when an entrepreneur succeeds?

In the initial stages before success, he or she supplies brains, energy, initiative, and someone else usually supplies the money. But now he has the money as well.

Does he become an investor? Or does he seek another challenge?

Does he continue to develop his original project? Or does he retire to write a book?

Roger Shashoua belongs mainly to the second category. 'People without dreams' he tells us, 'are like birds without wings.' For him, therefore, once the thrill of the chase is over, boredom will set in. The hare hates the thought of becoming a tortoise.

But is that rational?

The greatest difficulty that Roger has faced is not entrepreneurship, but with après entrepreneurship. Only then does the restless impatience, which has carried him to the summit of success, become his enemy. The skill in becoming a successful investor is the opposite to that of the serial entrepreneur, which he is.

In his pursuit of constant action, the serial entrepreneur ignores the eighth wonder of the world – the effect of compound growth. A thousand dollars invested in Berkshire Hathaway 50 years ago would be worth around US$300 million today, although admittedly this is an extreme case (and there would have been no frictional costs from tax, or from paying off greedy merchant bankers).

I do not believe that the pursuit of riches is Shashoua's main driving force. I think that the explication in his case is temperamental, not rational. Rather, there is within him a low boredom threshold, a longing for something new, and a furious impatience with anything old.

Impatience is one of the most obvious qualities of this multi-faceted man. 'What is Shashoua like?' I asked the stockbroker who fixed up our first meeting five years ago. 'He does not have much time for fools', he replied unhelpfully – since presumably he was not referring to himself.

The quality that comes across from the first moment is an amazing verbal fluency, like an 'always on' radio, which makes the idea of his writing a book – let alone two – unlikely.

But what a programme!

There are many – too many – books on business by entrepreneurs. Normally, they recite a seemingly inevitable Horatio Alger-like climb up the ladder of success. Roger tells an altogether more honest, and far more absorbing tale of his career to date, strewn with the need to overcome daunting and hidden obstacles.

If you placed Roger Shashoua on a desert island, it would only be a matter of days before he had started trading with the natives, had struck up a close relationship with the local chief and probably married the chief's daughter.

Today, the terrains of his choice – Russia and Eastern Europe – are altogether more treacherous than our increasingly legalistic West. The frontier between entrepreneurism and piracy is – to say the least – blurred, with few laws to rely on. In these places, therefore, the law of mutual advantage is the one on which to rely. So, exceptional doses of perseverance, boldness and ingenuity are required for success. And Roger Shashoua has these in buckets.

His idea that for every problem there must be a solution is exactly the opposite of the critical-thinking-argument culture in which the West is saturated. Central to his success is his quality of instant empathy with people in many different cultures, including a multitude of women.

The ability to immediately place himself in the shoes of a another party – possibly a competitor or adversary – and to improvise more or less instantly a solution that will benefit all sides has to be seen to be believed.

And it can be seen in this book*.

This skill, which is so rare in most of us, is second nature to him.

The Shashoua family comes from the same Iraqi village near the Tigris that has exported to Britain such brilliant business brains as the Saatchis, Jack Dellal and the Zilkas. Was it something in the water supply?

Among the many stories that he tells in this book, there is one of international significance which, as far as I know, has never even been hinted at before. Through his friendship with Zhao Ziyang, the Chinese leader of the 1980s, he learnt that the Chinese were flabbergasted by the British offer to hand over Hong Kong early for nothing. At the very least, they expected a substantial trade-off and, incredibly, were even ready to consider sharing power with Britain permanently.

In dealing with Roger Shashoua, following him around the world, usually well off the beaten track to places like Delhi, Agadir, Bombay, Casablanca, Yekatrinberg, Volgagrad or Belgrade†, I have frequently been exasperated, confused and exhausted but never, for a moment, bored.

Given the character of 'our hero' that I have attempted to describe above, this entertaining book that follows on from 'The

---

*   See in particular Chapter 11

†   I should mention here that Roger's grasp of geography is notoriously shaky. Those along for the ride should bring their own map.

Paper Millionaire' can only be the second of several likely future volumes – an interim report, if you like.

Nicholas Berry

Nicholas Berry is an investor and publisher. His family interests include Mintel International, the Anglo American research business, Intersport Psc in Switzerland and Stancroft Trust. They were formerly owners of the London Daily Telegraph.

Prologue

This story starts while I was in an unaccustomed period of limbo in 1988. I had been frozen out of the chairmanship and control of ICE Group Plc, the international exhibition management group which I had founded in the UK. At the time, ICE had acquired options from the London Docklands Development Corporation (LDDC), in partnership with the Chinese Tianjin Municipal People's Government, to develop a US$400-million Chinese Trade and Cultural Centre in the heart of London's Docklands. The full story of that project and its fate is detailed in the final chapter of this book, covering the three emerging markets of greatest opportunity for entrepreneurs. However, the saga of the China Trade and Cultural Centre venture represents only a small part of the development of my business career and philosophy and the roller-coaster ride of my life for its first 40 years.

I was brought up and educated in Egypt by my mother, a noted Beirut beauty and, until she was widowed, by my father, the elder son of the house of Shashoua, one of Iraq's three leading Jewish business families, who had migrated to Egypt before World War II. We had survived the change of regime from King Farouk to President Nasser without persecution but the family fortune and status had dwindled.

From childhood, my mother had allocated to me, as her elder son, the then improbable task of recovering the family's status and wealth and at the age of 16 I was shipped off to the USA to fulfil my destiny. Having gained a place at the University of Illinois, I pursued as fully as I could my entrepreneurial talents in order to make ends meet, while exploring the 'groves of Academe' with a succession of charming female companions. In the meantime, my mother, my most constant supporter and critic, could not understand why it was taking me so long to make my first US$1 million.

I started out as an inventor and built the largest patent licensing agency – Patents International Group in the USA. It was during this time that the amazing growth potential of the exhibition and events industry first struck me. Instead of selling licences and patents at trade shows, I realised that one could easily 'package air' into a sellable commodity, like bottled water, and distribute it as a desirable and essential product worldwide.

This 'air' was packaged in the form of rented space, bare space, dressed with a theme and marketed according to the void it was filling. So I set out for the Middle East to places such as Kuwait and Saudi Arabia, where I established my own trade shows in construction, motoring, fashion, medicine, telecommunications, food and travel to name a few. We provided an opportunity for international companies to 'test' the waters in these new markets, while bringing foreign investment opportunities in return.

The concept proved successful beyond my initial expectations. Our company, Middle East Trade & Exhibitions, grew into the largest private exhibition organizer in the Middle East & Gulf region. As it grew, I needed a further challenge. Always looking for my 'next fix', I decided to venture into the untapped markets of Africa.

During the mid-80s through to the 1990s, I shifted our business interests south from the Middle East down to Central Africa, organising events in Nigeria and the Ivory Coast, in fields such as oil and gas. Again, we struck 'gold', finding that no one else had managed to successfully navigate these 'virgin' territories, facilitating international business opportunities on a global level.

In 1982, I approached China as my next challenge, seeking to conquer yet another foreign market. We produced the first-ever private international Manufacturing, Technology and Product Exhibition in Beijing at a time when trade events were run solely by the Chinese Government. In time, ICE Group became the largest private international trade fair organiser in China, running up to 60 exhibitions a year in cities such as Beijing, Shanghai, Shenzen and Tianjin.

My endless quest for a challenge continued. There still remained a considerable lack of modern exhibition facilities in China at the time, with most shows being held in special purpose-built state-run buildings. In partnership with local authorities, such as the Shenzen and Tianjin municipal governments, we were able to build state-of-the-art exhibition facilities, which raised the profile of our events to a whole new level. As these centres were established, the flow of foreign companies entering these markets started to gather pace.

The exhibition industry proved to be an exhilarating opportunity for travel, face-to-face contact and business encounters with boundless commercial growth. The risk ratio proved extremely small compared to the rewards we reaped. As our events and themes grew, so did our expansion into new and untapped markets.

Along the way, and through many adventures, I made and lost fortunes several times, learning, sometimes to my cost, the differences between the exhilarating but erratic flight path of a 'serial entrepreneur', and the less spectacular accumulation of more tangible assets by the establishment.

With the profits from a series of property assets taken in 1987, I had now accumulated some $20 million in cash. I had survived the stock market crash of that year, but I was a 'paper millionaire' without paper and without a vehicle for my next adventure into entrepreneurial outer space. However, there were many blessings to count in my personal life, with a fine family and financial security for them.

Perhaps the most satisfying aspect of my new 'retired paper millionaire' status was that my mother finally declared that I had reached the end of the task that she had set me more than 30 years before. 'You are a millionaire when you don't need to work. A millionaire, my son, is a man who helps the people who have helped him, lives in a penthouse, and is written about in the gossip columns'. I was still some years away from being in the gossip columns, although I had the doubtful distinction of being the model for a character in Tom Wolfe's acclaimed novel '*A Man in Full*'. However, the rest of her definition had come true.

Although the sum of these blessings brought satisfaction, they did not deliver contentment. Entrepreneurs are dreamers and paper millionaires are not quitters. They are driven to make it and as one dream fades another is created. Like many of the other characters who pass through the pages that follow, fresh dreams and pastures new took me into more adventures and as much success as any serial entrepreneur could reasonably expect.

Chapter 1

The Wonderful World of Publishing?

UNTIL I sat down to write my first book, my exposure to book publishing had been limited, but I was to learn very quickly that publishing entrepreneurs are a species apart from the successful business people that I had encountered in my career to date. Writing the book was a creative but taxing exercise, which I thoroughly enjoyed. I had an obsessive need to communicate all the hard lessons that I had learned up to that point in my pursuit of paper millions while the victories and defeats were still fresh in my mind. I soon found that the publication of the book was a task of a quite different order.

Most authors, even those with literary talent as yet unknown, are familiar with the regular return of their manuscripts with rejection slips as they thud through their letterboxes on to the door mat, and I was determined to avoid such a discouraging experience. With this in mind, I decided that the best way to get published was to find a smaller prestigious house run by its publisher-owner who was at least as eccentric as myself. I was fortunate to be introduced to Colin Haycraft, the owner of Gerald Duckworth & Co Ltd, who ran his publishing house from The Old Piano Factory, Gloucester Crescent, in London NW1. Founded in 1899, with its well-known Duck logo, Duckworth was an unusual publishing house, which reflected the character of its owner. Colin, with a First Class Oxford Honours Degree, was a charming but unassuming man and a fine publisher, being one of the very few to edit, as well as publish, many of his books, in addition to being an author in his own right.

Colin and I got on well from the moment we met and became great friends. He was intrigued by the totally unfamiliar business world that I inhabited, attracted to the notion of paper million-aires and amused by my experiences. There was just one problem, he explained, for Duckworth in publishing my book – I was a total unknown to the reading public. "Authors need to be famous, academically qualified or dead for their books to sell", he said, "and you, my dear Roger, are none of these."

Putting aside the third alternative, I set about acquiring aca-demic credentials. I already held visiting Professorships in the Republic of China and South Korea. Now, I was able to acquire an Honorary Fellowship at North East Polytechnic and was asso-ciated with Imperial College.

After six months, I was able to return to Colin and place before him the evidence of my academic respectability. Colin relented. "I'll publish your book," he said "although I've never published anything like this before."

By now, after many convivial evenings with Colin, I came to understand the commercial realities of publishing. Therefore, when signing up with Duckworth, I asked if I might help in the marketing of the book. Colin accepted the suggestion willingly.

While the book was being edited and printed, I concentrated on developing the marketing and public relations campaigns. The promotional tool that gave me the most fun and also attracted the most publicity was the song *I'm a Paper Millionaire*, written for me by a taxi driver friend who was also a part-time songwriter. The song, available as a record or tape was promoted in the advance publicity, together with the book, the game and the play.

The making of the record was also my first encounter with Richard Branson. In 1988, our office was next door to Richard's. Whereas we had a small office building and a large off-road parking area, he had a large office building and a tiny parking space. Quite often Branson cars were parked on Shashoua territory but we responded by placing good-humoured notes on the windshields. It was time to ask Richard's people for a return gesture, and they helped me to locate the singer for my song, an up-and-coming soul sister. *I'm a Paper Millionaire* never hit the charts but we sold several hundred tapes and it still echoes in my – if no one else's – ears.

Selling the book into the trade took my utmost selling skills and persistence, finally gaining access to the senior buyers of W H Smith and Waterstone's. I made it into their outlets by pestering the managers of their major stores in the London area to 'support a local author' and gained their acceptance to stock the book there and in airport outlets. The independent booksellers in the different boroughs of London from Chelsea and Kensington to Hampstead and Highgate had to be approached individually. However, they also responded to the 'support your local author' theme, although my claim to local residence was somewhat stretched.

As well as promoting the forthcoming book, I also set out to raise the public profile of Duckworth itself by attracting general media attention. The most memorable event which certainly achieved coverage in the daily press was The Duckling Ball, a giant children's party staged in London at the Hammersmith Palais one Sunday in September 1989.

'Le Palais' was a well-known venue for rave parties, pop concerts and Saturday night dancing. Organized by Duckworth Group under the slogan 'Our first duty to children is to make them happy', the event attracted support from all the main children's charities, to which the takings were donated.

The centrepiece of the Duckling Ball was a guest star appearance of 'Count Duckula' – a TV cartoon character much in vogue at the time, who rocked and rolled on stage under the spotlights.

More than anything else, the Duckling Ball was sponsored by a host of well-know global and UK brand names, ranging from American Express, British Airports Authority, BMW, British Airways and Coca Cola to Hertz, Marks & Spencer and Texaco. Thanks to their generous donations, the Duckling Ball made a worthwhile contribution to charity. Colin was somewhat dazed by the sudden publicity and the unlikely association of Count Duckula with his beloved Duck.

The launch date for *The Paper Millionaire* was 27 October 1989 and I was booked for interviews on television and radio throughout the week of the launch.

Early printed copies of *The Paper Millionaire* were made available just in time for the 1988 Frankfurt Book Fair – the world's largest annual international trade show for publishers and the leading marketplace for trading in foreign language printing rights.

However, booking space at the 1988 Book Fair in the British publishers Hall – even six months ahead – proved more difficult than I expected. Duckworth, who had the status of an accredited publisher, was grudgingly awarded a space of just 6 square metres, which I described as 'a f****** mousehole.' This was the first of many clashes with Pieter Weidhaas – the Managing Director of the Frankfurt Book Fair – and his team in a foretaste of our long-running battle to control, organize and manage book fairs across Central and Eastern Europe.

Fortunately, my micro-stand was next to the large and well-populated exhibit of Transworld, one of the global market leaders in the publication of English-language fiction in the USA and the UK. There were plenty of visitors to the Transworld stand and I was determined to capture their attention. The soul sister who had recorded my jingle sportingly agreed to be flown over from London to Frankfurt in time for the opening. A lady of ample proportions, she was positioned somewhat precariously on a box at the front of my stand with microphone, amplifier and a backing tape, from where she belted out *'I need a Paper Millionaire, give me a cash injection and I'll play the wildest game…'* all day, with short intervals for rest and recuperation.

At the end of the second day, the Transworld Marketing Director came over to me and said 'If I have to hear that bloody jingle one more time, don't be surprised if I complain formally to the organizers of the show.' However, the complaint was good-humoured and I was happy to tone down the singing. The publicity stunt had worked. By the end of the fair I had signed several lucrative foreign rights deals.

During the four days of the show I ventured out of my mouse-hole some of the time and, by visiting many of the stands, was able to gain a firsthand impression of the range and quality of offerings from the various publishing houses. One of the stands that I singled out specifically was that of *The Bookseller*, the premier weekly journal of the British publishing establishment. At my most charming, I explained who I was and asked the lady there if *The Bookseller* would consider reviewing my book. Not unkindly, I was told that 'There are 50,000 English language books published every year and you are a completely unknown author. There is no possibility that we would read, let alone review your book.' 'In that case,' I said, 'I would like to place a full colour double page spread advert in the next edition possible to publicize *The Paper Millionaire* and seven other Duckworth titles.' This time, the reply was still more dismissive. 'Our advertising space is fully sold out for the next eight issues, so we can't accept an advertisement for your book.' I concluded that *The Bookseller* must be very profitable to take such a complacent stance and that this was one sector of publishing where there was surely room for competition.

In light of my own international exhibition experience, the overriding conclusion that I drew from the sold-out Frankfurt Fair was that international book fairs were highly profitable

enterprises. Were there other opportunities, I wondered, for developing new book fairs in other countries of Europe?

The marketing blitz which spearheaded *The Paper Millionaire'*
paid off – the media campaign had created public interest and
shown the book trade that there was promotional support for the
book. With W H Smith now stocking the book, Duckworth sold
8,500 hard cover copies, making it a bestseller in their terms.
Colin Haycraft was delighted.

Based on our good personal relationship, I offered to invest
new capital in Gerald Duckworth & Co Ltd for a 50 per cent
interest. I also offered the procurement of additional working
capital as and when necessary, on the understanding that Colin
could buy back my shares from me at any time in the future at his
option, if he decided that he wanted to terminate the partnership.
Colin would continue to run the core business as managing director without interference and I would focus on marketing, brand
management, acquisition of new authors and titles and diversifi-
cation in the publishing arena.

Immediately following my investment, we booked a stand for
Duckworth at the Spring 1989 London Book Fair at which the
'new Duckworth Group' would be launched. We advertised for
new authors in the trade press and by circulating flyers under the
banner headline 'Come to Duckworth.' The publicity and networking generated a clutch of important new titles. Among them
was *Collapse of the Soviet Union* – a prophetic work starting
with Mikhail Gorbachev's rise to power and anticipating the
Velvet Revolution in the then Czechoslovakia, the destruction of
the Berlin Wall and the domino effect throughout Central and
Eastern Europe of the liberation from communist regimes. That
book also became a Duckworth bestseller. The London Book Fair
1989 brought further success for Duckworth, raising the profile
of the imprint and bringing scores of visitors and friends of Colin

from within the industry, who were delighted to find that this Duck was far from dead.

I studied the calendar of some 20 book fair events held internationally and became further aware of the void that existed in certain untapped markets.

I also became increasingly aware of the editorial weaknesses of *The Bookseller* magazine. Its prosperity was heavily dependent on advertising revenue from major American and British publishing groups and reviews were heavily concentrated on their books, to the disadvantage of smaller independent publishers, for whose smaller number of new titles a review was a critical marketing channel to the book trade. Certainly, in Duckworth's case, *The Bookseller* provided no support.

Curiously, *The Bookseller* appeared to pay scant attention to what was happening in the European Union (EU) and other parts of Western Europe. There was also no recognition of the early signs of the re-awakening involvement of authors and publishers from Eastern Europe with the West, which offered an opportunity for another type of publishing journal.

And so my concept of *European Bookseller* was born. Its constituency would be English language booksellers throughout Western and Eastern Europe. Editorial would focus on pan-European issues and on book trade and publishing industry developments in individual European markets and selected International Book Trade Exhibitions, which it would preview.

European Bookseller was launched on an unsuspecting publishing world at the 1989 Frankfurt Book Fair. The main thrust of our marketing drive at Frankfurt would be to brief publishers, market test the concept and solicit advertisers and editorial contributors for the first edition.

Our reception at Frankfurt exceeded all expectations. It was clear that we had a potentially winning formula and, if we could translate the promises of support into advertising over the next few months, the first issue planned for March might even show an operating profit.

After Frankfurt, I solicited advertisements from all the 70 or so book fairs around the world. David Costello, a former Macmillan sales manager, joined us to sell into his network of UK publishers and book distribution chains. To ensure that *European Bookseller* received maximum publicity prior to its launch, I offered to co-sponsor the British Book Awards – a kind of Oscar for less literary authors than those who contended for the Booker Prize. The organizer and promoter of the awards dinner at the Park Lane Hotel in London in January 1990 was *Publishing News*. Fred Newman, the Editor, was a firm supporter of *European Bookseller* from its earliest days, unlike *The Bookseller*, which remained aloof in the face of approaches to co-operate and became actively hostile as we progressed.

The awards dinner was attended by 500 of the great, the good and the less good in the publishing world. Presentation speeches were given throughout the evening by well-known authors and publishing luminaries. The nine awards took the form of elegant brass nib-shaped sculptures gratuitously christened 'nibbies' and *European Bookseller* sponsored the Book Promotion of the Year. The presenters included the novelists Jilly Cooper, and Jeffrey Archer, whose reply to an ignorant bookseller's question 'Do you earn more than £10,000?' of 'Some days I do, some days I don't' caused some hilarity. Among the prize winners were HRH the Prince of Wales as Author of the Year for his controversial book, *A Vision of Britain* and Roald Dahl as Children's Author of the year. The *European Bookseller of the Year* award went to Sphere Publishing for their promotion of Ben Elton's *Stark*; for a campaign costing £4,000, the book went to number one in the British bestseller list and sold 450,000 copies. The event certainly gave *European Bookseller* a high profile before the first issue even appeared and illustrated one of the pillars of my business philosophy – 'Start at the top.'

The first issue of *European Bookseller* two months later was a *tour de force*. It ran to 136 pages and contained interviews with the then cream of the publishing world. The distribution and publishing services sector were also among our advertisers.

The April edition, which extended to 150 pages, was published at the end of March just in time for distribution at the London International Book Fair at which Duckworth and *European Bookseller* took a combined stand. The positive reaction to Duckworth and *European Bookseller* at the London International Book Fair from fellow exhibitors confirmed that we were now a recognized force on the English-language publishing scene.

At about this time, Duckworth's annual accounts for the first year of my involvement were published, showing a handsome profit of several hundred thousand pounds – the first for many years. I had expected Colin Haycraft to be pleased but his reaction surprised me. 'Roger,' he said. 'This is terrible news. I have to speak to you urgently.' What could be the problem? 'All these authors who have written for me for years without payment,' he explained 'are now asking me for back royalties. We are ruined.' Not unreasonably, those who had laboured without reward from loyalty and affection to Colin, helping to keep Duckworth afloat in its lean years, now felt that they could claim their dues. I calmed Colin down, met with the most clamorous authors myself and reached an amicable agreement with each one individually, although Duckworth's patient bank manager had to accept an unexpected dent in cash flow. Aside from this minor crisis, Duckworth's affairs proceeded according to plan and I was able to continue devoting my attention to *European Bookseller* and international book fairs.

Chapter 2

International Book Fairs Beckon

My visit to the Frankfurt Book Fair had rekindled an appetite for an active involvement in international trade fairs and the Frankfurt experience had opened my eyes as to how profitable a well-organized annual international book fair could be.

I felt that there were two criteria that I must satisfy if my foray into international book fairs was to succeed. First, I must come up with a theme and rationale that would give my event a unique appeal. Second, the location must be a prestigious major city with a long history of culture and civilisation, attractive to exhibitors and attendees alike.

The theme I chose initially was the cause of promoting the EU and the celebration of a united Europe. By mid-1990, I was able to add a new and much more powerful strand to that theme – the re-emergence of literature and publishing from Central & Eastern Europe and Russia too. Thus, I was able to present the *1er Salon du Livre et de la Culture Européene* to the world as the first event at which the publishers and authors from all these countries would attend as exhibitors and participate in a round table conference on the future of European publishing. Nor would Russia be excluded, as attitudes to doing business with Russia had softened markedly.

The choice of Paris as the location for my book fair was not difficult. France had an almost unbroken history as the intellectual and artistic leader of Europe and Paris was the ideal city to host the *Salon International du Livre*. The other attraction of locating the event in Paris was that it would give British and American publishers the chance to exhibit their English language titles there for the first time, having been excluded for so long from participation in the established *Salon du Livre* by France's Syndicat National de l'Edition.

Having settled on Paris as the location, I realised that for any initiative to have a reasonable chance of success, diplomacy at the highest level was required and we planned our approach carefully in the autumn of 1989.

My starting point was my wife's cousin – the film star Roger Hanin – who was married to the sister of President François Mitterand's wife. Through this connection we met Jacques Lang, France's Minister of Culture, for a drink at Fouquet's and were able to enlist his warm support for our approach to the Syndicat National de l'Edition. We had high hopes that his endorsement would give us the key to that Bastille of French publishing.

However, we were ill-prepared for *la France chauviniste*. We were received politely enough by Alain Grund, the President, and members of the Syndicat committee. After assuring my audience that I regarded France as my second and cultural home, I plunged into my prepared presentation in my best formal French.

'Messieurs et Mesdames, I would like to offer the Syndicat the opportunity to take the cultural lead for French publishing in a celebration of united Europe's literature. This is your cultural right and the assembly of all free Europe's publishers, including English-language publishing houses, in a single exhibition in Paris would confirm France's pre-eminence. I propose the addition of a Salon International to your Salon du Livre or, if you prefer, as a separate event at another time for which we would take complete financial responsibility.'

My statement was received impassively and the reply delivered by Alain Grund with that *froideur* in which the French excel left no doubt that their co-operation would not be forthcoming. The sole mission of the Syndicat National de l'Edition, we were told, was to further the cause of French-language publishing and French culture. In effect, *Adieu, Monsieur Shashoua* not *au revoir*. Nevertheless, their refusal gave no hint of the active opposition that would follow.

Reviewing our position, I decided to go it alone, without the Syndicat. Booking space at the Grand Palais proved impossible because the Syndicat had a stranglehold there on all literary events. We were told that there was no space available. Therefore, we sought an alternative venue and made a booking at the Parc des Expositions, Porte de Versailles in the name of *1er Salon International du Livre et de la Culture Européene* for 14–17 February 1991. Not surprisingly perhaps, the Syndicat regarded our action as extreme provocation and eight weeks later made representations to Parc des Expositions, which cancelled our reservation. The booking was restored only after the intervention of our lawyers.

By the time the second issue of *European Bookseller* was published, opportunities were now emerging for book fair initiatives within Central and Eastern Europe. Foremost among these were the Czech Republic, Hungary, Romania and Poland with the Czech Republic very much in the vanguard. Not only was Vaclav Havel – himself an internationally celebrated author – now President, but there was a long and honourable history of Czech publishers continuing to publish throughout the long years of the communist regime.

By December 1989, Vaclav Havel was able to declare the integration of the independent *samizdat* publishers as an accredited part of the Czech publishing industry in an article titled *Goodbye samizdat!* (the underground publishing movement). By mid-1990, the face of Czech publishing was transformed.

Many new organizations, individuals and informal groups registered with the authorities as future new publishers. By 31 May 1990, 370 publishing permits had been issued. The copyright regime also became more favourable to authors who were also liberated. They were now free to negotiate for themselves with any publisher. Likewise, publishers could approach any author whose work they wished to publish.

These new found freedoms provided the perfect conditions for the launch of an international book fair and writers' festival in Prague, Czech Republic. There was an enthusiastic response from Karel Srp, the new Director of Books and Publishing at the Ministry, and the first reaction from the Czech Minister of Culture – Dr Milan Uhde – was similarly positive. Milan Uhde was himself an acclaimed poet, prose author and playwright, whose stage and radio plays were performed widely outside Czechoslovakia. Provisional dates were agreed for May 1991 for the 1st Prague International Book Fair and Writers Festival to be sponsored and co-organized by the Ministry of Culture in the Palace of Culture.

The agreement required the President's approval and we were granted an informal audience at the castle with President Havel, who declared his firm support and readily agreed to write an open letter of endorsement for publication with the announcement of the Book Fair. The dates of 23–26 May 1991 were finalized for the event; Karel Srp was nominated as co-organizer.

However, the path to the announcement was stonier than we anticipated. Just as we were congratulating ourselves on a mission accomplished, news came from Karel Srp that the Minister, Dr Uhde, had decided to cancel the Book Fair. We found out that he had been approached by the Frankfurt Book Fair in alliance with the Syndicat National des Editions in Paris, with an offer to stage a book fair in our place to which they would devote their combined resources, ensuring that the cream of Western publishing houses would attend. Fortunately, we now had President Havel's signed letter endorsing our Book Fair which we hastened to publish in the July/August edition of *European Bookseller,* together with the formal announcement of the 1st Prague International Book Fair and Writers Festival as a double-page spread. In the face of publication, Minister Uhde had no alternative but to withdraw the cancellation notice. The event was definitely on and we proceeded to work through Karel Srp with the Ministry of Culture to ensure that it would be a success.

Consequently, by the end of June 1990, we had two book fairs in Paris and Prague confirmed for the following year and I felt that we had made a good start on penetrating the profitable European book fair market.

With all this excitement and the concentration of my efforts on securing the two book fairs, I paid less attention to the book publishing affairs of Duckworth than perhaps I should have. Towards the end of June, Colin Haycraft came to see me in some embarrassment. 'Roger,' he said, 'I don't think I can stand the pace of Duckworth Group development any more in these strange new areas which are far beyond my experience and which I don't really understand. I'm very grateful to you for what you have done, but would you be willing to sell your shareholding in Gerald Duckworth & Co Limited?' It seems that an old friend – one of Colin's tennis partners – and a director of a major City bank, had suggested buying my shares as an investment for his son in his 20s who was keen to become a publisher and would like to work under Colin's direction. I asked Colin to consider carefully whether he really wanted to change partners and, when he confirmed that this was so, released my shares to him as I had always promised.

Unfortunately, events did not turn out as Colin expected. Within six months, the Old Piano Factory was put on sale forcing Colin out of the company. This was a tragic end to a fine publisher and original character for whom Duckworth had been his *raison d'être*. Soon afterwards, Colin died suddenly of a heart attack.

Chapter 3

Hello Moscow – Adieu Paris

Following the sale of my shares in Duckworth, I changed the name of Duckworth Group to The Avencourt Group, which now comprised of *European Bookseller* and Avencourt Exhibitions divisions.

From July onwards, the marketing focus of our sales team was re-directed to attracting exhibitors for the Paris *Salon International du Livre* and the Prague International Book Fair in that order, while maintaining the advertising sales drive for *European Bookseller*. On the horizon too was the prospect of book fairs in Bucharest, Warsaw and Moscow, which we began to consider as the sequels to the Prague Book Fair and Writers' Festival.

At this stage, I positioned the *Salon International du Livre* in Paris at the Porte de Versailles in our marketing as the principal event of 'The Paris Book Festival', which was to include three additional new events at CNIT Congress Hall (la Défense). These events were: a Writers' Festival, a conference on the key issues facing the European Book Industry and the European Book Awards and Gala Evening. The writers' festival was intended to be a low-key occasion for writers, publishers and literary agents from every country attending to meet in a relaxed ambiance. In contrast, the European Book Awards would be modelled on the

British Book Awards and were conceived as international literature's equivalent of the Cannes Film Festival or MIDEM (the Paris
Music Festival), with a black tie gala dinner and TV coverage.
Nomination forms for the European Book Awards were published
for the first time in the September edition of *European Bookseller*.
Throughout the summer and autumn of 1990 *European Bookseller* continued to establish itself as the dominant provider of
publishing and book trade news and information for Europe.

It was soon time for the Frankfurt Book Fair, as October came
around again. We had started to gather bookings for the Paris
Salon International du Livre the following February from British
publishers but the level of interest from the USA remained low.
While the Avencourt team continued to press our established contacts during the Fair for bookings to both the Paris and Prague
events, the main thrust of my efforts this time was to woo the
representatives of publishers' associations and publishing houses
from the Central & Eastern Europe (CEE) countries.

I also had my mind set on securing a major Russian presence,
which would add greatly to the attraction of the Paris Book Festival. Their participation would give their Western counterpart the
opportunity to talk business with them outside the confines of
Moscow and government scrutiny.

The immediate reciprocity that we could offer the Russians was
made at the Frankfurt Book Fair, which was attended by Marat V
Shishigin, President of the powerful Soviet Publishers Association
(SPA) and his aides. The SPA had been set up as recently as April
1990 at the All-Union Publishers' Congress and its formation was
a logical outcome of *perestroika*. Together, the members published
about 2 billion books annually, amounting to three-quarters of all
books published in the USSR. A meeting between us was arranged
and we found immediate common ground. Marat Shishigin was
intent on developing the international standing of the SPA as the

new face of Russian publishing and recognized the value that attendance at the Paris Book Festival could bring in accelerating the achievement of his objective. For my part, the SPA was the crucial channel and the best way to ensure a strong Russian presence in Paris.

As a follow-up to this congenial first meeting it was agreed that Jonathan Reuvid – Editor of *European Bookseller* – and I should visit Moscow in November at the invitation of the SPA.

The Moscow trip was an eye-opener for us. Alarmed by stories of the primitive condition of Russian hotels and fond of his creature comforts, Jonathan insisted on packing his own bathplug. He was, therefore, pleasantly surprised to find that there was constant hot and cold water in his bathroom, as well as a plug, when we checked in at the Hotel Rossiya at the foot of Red Square opposite St Basil's.

During our visit, we paid courtesy calls on the directors of VAA, the state copyright agency, and the Moscow Book Fair. The directors of both organizations proved to be worldly-wise cosmopolitans and both VAA and the Moscow Book Fair gave assurances of their support for the Paris Book Festival.

The mood in Moscow that autumn was almost relaxed, with an undercurrent of excitement pervading the city. *Perestroika* had brought a new air of confidence, which had infected most of the people in publishing that Jonathan and I met and even people in the street, except, it seemed, the door staff in hotels whose mission was definitely not to make foreign visitors welcome. Marat Shishigin hosted a lavish dinner for us at the Artist's Club, where luminaries of the Russian stage and screen jostled with artists and the cream of the literary world. President Reagan had been entertained there during his recent visit to Moscow. At one publisher's lunch at a well-known restaurant decorated in *fin de siècle* red plush, Jonathan was seated next to an ex-KGB man, uncertain of his future, who had accompanied Russian publishers in their visits to the West in sterner times. 'I have been to London in 1974' he confided. 'Guest of Robert Maxell. We stayed at Claridge's Hotel.

One of our party fell out of top floor bedroom window.' 'How did that happen?' Jonathan asked. 'He was careless,' came the laconic reply.

Three weeks later, I flew to Moscow to confirm terms and arrangements with the SPA for a delegation of Russian publishing houses to exhibit at the Paris Book Festival. The highlight of that visit was a dinner in the Kremlin with Archbishop Pitirim, the Metropolitan Archbishop of Volokolmask and Yuriyev, who was also Director of the Publishing Department of the Patriarchate and had been chosen to lead the delegation to Paris. As we sat at dinner in the dimly lit ornate barrel-vaulted room, I felt that it could have been a film set for Eisenstein's *Ivan the Terrible*. The archbishop was a confidant of Mikhail Gorbachev so I came away feeling that the SPA publishers' attendance at the Paris Book Festival had the Presidential blessing.

On this trip I also made the acquaintance with Mikhail ('Misha'), the young technocrat who had been assigned to the SPA as Marat Shishigin's aide. He was our main point of contact and acted as liaison officer with SPA's publishing house members. As we got to know him better, I discovered that he was a member of that elite club, known as the 'Komsamol', to which only the brightest graduates of the USSR's universities and academies belonged.

We soon grew to depend on Misha as our 'Mr Fix-it' in the lead-up to the Paris Book Festival. Subsequently, he became a close associate, playing a key role in my further adventures in Russia.

At the turn of the year, my enemies in Paris struck again. An edict was issued by the Syndicat National des Editions to its publisher members forbidding them to take stands at the *Salon International du Livre* in February. The instruction was followed to the letter and the news spread rapidly to British and American publishers, many of whom developed cold feet. The French boycott was hugely damaging, if French publishers would not support an international book fair in their own capital city. English language publishers, German, Spanish, Dutch and Scandinavian publishing houses took the same view and decided to stay at home. We had failed to breach the Bastille of French publishing but there was still the prospect that French booksellers and members of the reading public would attend the event in order to view and become acquainted with the new books and publishers of Russia and Eastern Europe.

The final blow came when I received a call from the editor of *Livres Hebdo*. 'Roger, *je suis desolé,*' he said. 'I regret that I must cancel your space booking, and I shall be unable to report on your International Book Festival. My regular advertisers, such as Hachette, have told me that if we support your event they will cancel their advertising schedules for the next six months. Without their insertions, my journal is dead.' I had to agree that there was nothing else he could do. After August 1990, *European Bookseller* received no further advertisements from French publishers.

In spite of these body blows, my resolve held firm and I was still determined to make the *Salon International du Livre* a success. The bookings from Russia and the CEE countries held firm and there were no further cancellations from the few remaining Western publishers and book service providers who had signed up.

By contrast, arrangements for the 1st Prague International Book Fair and Writers' Festival were going forward according to plan. After the initial glitch, the Minister of Culture's antipathy was transformed to full support. Bookings from Western publishing houses were more than anticipated and there was an intense interest in meeting the Czech writers whose works had been banned by the state for so long.

It seemed that the Writers' Festival was going to be the star attraction in Prague and I engaged Michael March, the British poet, translator and editor, as organizer. He was also the natural choice to direct the Writers' Festival in Paris, which preceded the Prague Festival. Behind the somewhat effete air of an archetypal poet which Michael cultivated assiduously was a keen commercial outlook, and I was grateful for his important contributions to both events.

From the latter part of 1990, I used the same tactics as for the Czech Republic of profiling the publishing industries of Romania, Hungary, Poland and later Bulgaria as the means of entry to their Ministries of Culture and any existing Book Fair organizations. The stratagem started to bear fruit in 1991, when we were able to announce in August the 1st Bucharest International Book Fair and Writers' Festival with the support of the Romanian Minister of Culture, a former opera singer, on the back of the successful event in Prague.

Throughout January 1991, we continued to battle with the logistics and administration for *Salon International du Livre* at the Porte de Versailles. The problem was rather one of spreading the exhibitors that we had over the 6,000 square metres of covered space to avoid drawing attention to the weak participation. The Russian delegation's exhibitors were given pride of place at the centre of the show.

The exhibitors spent 13 February in setting up their stands. I welcomed them individually and, exuding a confidence that we did not feel, spread cheer and encouragement. That evening we hosted a dinner at the local Sofitel for the delegations of writers from CEE countries who had checked in during the day. This was a happy occasion for them all, especially the two writers from Tallinn, who had only secured their exit visas that afternoon from the Russian immigration officials who still manned Estonia's borders. None of them had met before, although a few had corresponded. Also present at the dinner was the Metropolitan Archbishop Pitirim from Moscow, in a business suit, with his niece and a taciturn KGB 'minder'. Their presence caused some nervousness at first, especially among the Estonians, but everyone relaxed as the evening progressed. At the end of dinner, all the guests, including the KGB man, kissed the Archbishop's ring when he was the first to retire for the night.

The following morning, everyone was on their stands with the Archbishop now in his full regalia, mitre and staff, parading impressively at the front of the Patriarchate Publishing Department stand. The nakedness of the land was soon apparent. When the doors opened there was no flood of attendees. It was clear that the citizens of Paris were staying away in their thousands. The only excitement that occurred was a fire alert, which caused an invasion by the *pompiers* from the Paris Fire Department. They were welcomed by me, as they swelled attendance for a time. However, one exhibitor who was about to complete his only book sale of the day was less pleased when the fire alert caused his customer to depart in a hurry just as cash was about to change hands.

By the third day, exhibitors were resigned to their fate but remained remarkably good-tempered. As a thank you for their patience and understanding, I invited them all to a celebration dinner at a well-known restaurant at the top of Montmartre, which we took over for the evening. Food and wine flowed freely and a good time was had by all.

The *Salon International du Livre* had been a commercial disaster but our failure did not benefit French publishing. No one was in doubt as to the petty action of the Syndicat, which ruled it out of serious consideration as a force in international publishing for some years to come. On balance, our own reputation was enhanced; we had taken on the might of French chauvinism and had remained steadfast in the face of the boycott.

This saga was in sharp contrast to my experiences in Paris several years later when my subsequent exhibition company ITE booked the *Palais de Congrés* to stage the first all-Russian exhibition in Europe of Russian products, with 150 Russian companies participating. Francine, Head of the Conference Centre, was 36, beautiful, very seductive and married to a dentist. She had to be a powerful personality to maintain management control of the Conference centre. At that stage, I viewed myself as a 'non-entity' next to Francine but had to work closely with her to arrange conference dinners and other activities relating to the exhibition. I invited her for a drink; after about half an hour she decided that there was no point in going further, made her excuses very politely and left.

Three days later, I went to meet her for a business lunch at the Conference Centre. She was not there and her staff told me that there was no record of our supposed meeting. I was very angry with her for standing me up without notice, which was not a very 'French thing' to do. Besides, I simply wanted to do business and had no ulterior motive at that time. I could not believe that I had done anything to offend her.

I shunned the Conference Centre for a few days and then telephoned again. Francine herself answered the telephone, and I scolded her angrily for her behaviour. She apologized and claimed that, according to her diary, our lunch was in a week's time. On her insistence that we should make up. I invited her to a Russian delegation party in Montmartre. The Russians sang all evening and on into the night. Francine witnessed something completely outside her normal experience, had a great time and at 10.30 pm thanked me and took her leave.

Francine also attended the opening of the Russian exhibition in her capacity as Head of the Paris Conference Centre. I presented her with a gift-wrapped Cartier alarm clock, costing US$500, as a token of our appreciation. Jokingly, I suggested that the present would remind her of me and that perhaps we should go out together some time. Francine replied that if she was gong to have an affair with someone, I was the last person on earth with whom she would have one. She would make her own personal choice of a young Adonis.

Francine took the present home without opening it. At 4.00 am the next morning the alarm went off, but neither Francine nor her husband could imagine from where the loud ringing sound was coming. Eventually they traced it down to the gift-wrapped clock, which they duly silenced. Francine explained to her husband that the clock was a gift from a client.

The day after the exhibition finished, I was in the Conference Centre for the dismantling of the stands. Francine arrived on the scene and started laughing as she told me about the night's events. We went out to lunch and spent the afternoon making love.

The relationship with Francine was also one of the most fruitful for me in business terms. She tipped me off when the Russians were booking the Centre or when the Russian Minister of Commerce was paying a visit. Contact with him was especially useful because the Moscow ExpoCentre had by then opened an office in Paris. Through Francine, I knew months in advance when exhibitions were being planned. Moreover, she would bring me in as a sponsor, presenting me to the exhibition organizers as a *fait accompli* without the Russians even knowing. With Francine's help we were able to put on our security and aviation shows. Effectively, she acted as a lobbyist for ITE.

Francine became uncertain of her life in the future. She loved her husband, but she needed a male friend to whom she could talk. I invited her to join me in Moscow but she declined politely. She did visit Moscow once but did not relate to Russian women. I hadn't realized before that Francine might be jealous.

Returning to the *Salon International du Livre*, there was an unexpected consolation as we prepared to close. The representative of the Moscow Book Fair who had attended with the Russian delegation took me to one side to express its appreciation of the effort I had made on behalf of Russian publishers to give them public exposure to Western publishing. Would I like to consider taking on the role of co-organizer for the 1991 Moscow International Book Fair? If so, I was invited to visit Moscow as soon as possible for discussions.

Once again, the phoenix of my Trade Fair dreams had risen from the ashes of defeat.

Chapter 4

A Rookie In Russia

Returning to Russia in 1990 at the invitation of the Moscow Book Fair brought back to me vivid memories of my first visit in 1986, towards the end of the Cold War era. This was the period before Mikhail Gorbachev's doctrine of *perestroika* swept Central and Eastern Europe and lifted the heavy yoke of Moscow's domination of its satellite states and their command economies.

In 1986, Russia's ruler was Yuri Andropov, the former head of the KGB, who had seized power on the long-awaited demise of Leonid Brezhnev and was now installed in the Kremlin as Secretary General. There were few, if any, visible signs then of what was to come and how the iron grip of Communist Party rule would become relaxed under his successor. Our visit in 1986 was in the name of my old company, the ICE Group, of which Lord Wilson, the former Prime Minister, was then Chairman. It was entirely due to his connections and the high regard in which he was held by the Kremlin that the visit of our little delegation was made possible.

Our party consisted of Lord Wilson and myself, John Gooding – an associate dealing in property development who had worked with me on the London Docklands project, Roger Wilby – another director of ICE, and my cousin Jack Totah. Our mission in Russia was to look for opportunities there since our work in China, as described in the Prologue, was coming to an end. The trip was not without incident.

It got off to a bad start when we arrived at London Heathrow. Lord Wilson was met at the check-in by a senior member of airport courtesy staff and wafted off to the VIP lounge. The rest of us were told politely, but firmly, that we should register and proceed through immigration in the usual way. When it came to my turn, the check-in clerk, who had witnessed the VIP treatment of Lord Wilson and understood that we were in the same group, asked, 'Why is Harold Wilson going to Moscow?' Perhaps miffed by being shown the equivalent of 'the tradesman's entrance', I resorted to using my over-developed sense of humour. Leaning conspiratorially over the counter, I replied in a stage whisper 'Maybe he's defecting.' My quip was partly sparked off by the recent publication in Australia of *Spycatcher*, the memoirs of a disaffected middle-rank MI6 officer, which had caused wide public interest and no little embarrassment to the agency. There was also speculation at that time in the 'red top' press that Harold might be a Russian mole.

I should have realised that my joke, as well as being in poor taste, might not be considered funny by the professionals. On reaching immigration, I was met by two granite-faced plainclothes MI6 officers, who were definitely not amused and who marched me to a small windowless side room where I was interrogated at length. As a result, our flight to Moscow that morning was delayed and it took repeated assurances of my good conduct by my legal adviser from the City before I was released with a severe reprimand. Later, I was given a second dressing-down by the authorities in Moscow for wasting their time and had to promise that I would never do anything similar again.

In Moscow, we were assigned by Intourist to the prestigious National Hotel, where only guests of the Kremlin – rather than businessmen – normally stayed. We discovered during our visit that there was a secret passage between the hotel and the adjacent Intourist building. Of course, the reason for our accommodation was that there was a British ex-Prime Minister in our party. However, the so-called 'special relationship' between Harold Wilson and the British Labour Party with Russia should not be misunderstood. On the one hand, while it is true that the Russian Communist Party and the British Labour Party share *The Red Flag* as their conference signature tune, their definitions of 'socialism' are far apart and the Labour Party is firmly rooted in British democracy from its 19th-century foundation.

As for Lord Wilson, it is worth remembering that while he was friendly on a personal level with many communist heads of state, his closeness to Russia and Russia's high regard for him dated back to World War II. It was at this time that the yong Harold Wilson was President of the Board of Trade in Sir Winston Churchill's wartime government and played an important part in the delivery of supplies to the beleaguered Russians through the Baltic convoys. I worked for six years with Harold during the ICE era, benefited greatly from his enthusiastic support, enjoyed the warmth of his friendship and have no doubt that he was ever anything other than a firm British patriot.

During our 1986 visit we received nothing but courtesy from the Russian authorities but the attitude of the British Embassy in Moscow was ambivalent. While the Embassy staff formally supported Lord Wilson during the visit, they also did everything they could to neutralize him so that his presence did not interfere with the 'Iron Lady' policies of Margaret Thatcher's government.

We were taken by Intourist to visit a prime piece of real estate. At that time, Intourist was in charge of all tourist real estate development. The Russian Olympics were coming up and we were invited to consider building a hotel on a site on Olympisky Avenue. After careful deliberation we decided not to take up the invitation. I felt that the foreign investment climate in Russia at that time presented too many problems to take the risk. Having invested in China too early in its evolution from a command economy, I was not eager to make the same strategic mistake in Russia. In the end, another company built the hotel on Olympisky

Avenue. Ironically, five years later, it became the headquarters for many exhibition organizers, including those of my company, the ITE Group Plc.

If my first visit to Moscow was not a business success, it was certainly instructive and amusing. At the National Hotel our room had a radio with three plugs, which we thought was unusual. We decided to check out whether they were listening devices through the speakers of the hotel radio. Jack commented that 'it was a shame that we had forgotten to bring our umbrellas.' Later, when we descended to the lobby we were offered two umbrellas at the Reception.

Jack and I met two girls in Red Square who had a car. They invited us to their flat in the Moscow suburbs about one hour away from the centre. We had lunch together, listened to music and really appreciated the kindness of these two simple Russians – not at all what we were led to expect from the warnings we had received before we left for Moscow. Perhaps they were KGB agents, but they were lovely and sincerely hospitable people who wished us good luck, asking only to be sent an English-Russian dictionary, which we did on our return.

On another occasion while exploring Moscow on foot, Jack Totah and I were 'picked up' by two very attractive women who took us on a tour of the town. Along the way, we realized that they were possibly both KGB employees. When they decided that the two foreigners had no useful intelligence to divulge, we were dropped abruptly and had to find our own way back to the National Hotel. Ever with an eye to turning a quick profit, we found that exchanging hard currency for roubles with these ladies was a highly lucrative activity, but perhaps it was a set-up by the KGB. We found out subsequently that the roubles we had bought at three times the official rate were in large bills, while the official currency exchanges only issued roubles in small bills. In this way, foreigners who had bought roubles illegally were detected at the airport when they came to change back their roubles into hard currency. We avoided this trap by distributing lavish hospitality at the National, which provided nightly entertainment in the hotel ballroom. Our triple value high-denomination roubles stretched a long way in payment of our carousing.

Lord Wilson's accommodation was a suite of two double bedrooms with additional rooms for each member of our delegation. On each floor there was a control desk where a beautiful fat lady with gold teeth kept the room keys when hotel guests were away from their rooms. There was no way in which you could bring a lady friend into your room without bribing the keeper of the keys and we didn't try.

We had brought with us over 200 ballpoint pens with a string to put around the neck, which we gave out as souvenirs to doormen, bellboys and other hotel staff. In the next few days, we noticed that nearly all the staff at the hotel, in restaurants and elsewhere that we visited were wearing them – a clear signal that someone from our group had been there or had accorded a favour.

The British Embassy put a Rolls Royce at Lord Wilson's disposal but their tactic for keeping him out of circulation took the form of supplying two cases of Johnny Walker Black Label whisky to his room for his personal use. The tactic was successful and Lord Wilson made few appearances outside his suite. The 'neutralization' of Lord Wilson in this way worked to our advantage one night when we wanted to entertain guests and were able to use his suite while he was dozing for a romp with some girls whom we had met in the lobby bar.

At the hotel, we inevitably gravitated to the Philby Bar, where Roger Wilby was mistakenly paged as 'Mr Philby' without causing a single head to turn. The relaxed acceptance of Kim Philby – the most notorious of the British double agents who defected to Russia – as a Moscow citizen was in counterpoint to my MI6 experience at Heathrow on the way out. By then, Philby had been pensioned off as a full KGB colonel. We wondered how the treatment of Russian double agents fleeing to the US or the UK compared.

The Philby Bar was also the scene for my introduction to Tatiana, then working for the Moscow State Circus and the first of the Russian ladies who was to play such an important part in my education and experiences. Our rapport was immediate and we quickly became friends. During this first visit to Moscow, Tatiana went to visit her family and daughter and took me with her on an excursion well beyond the limits of the permitted zone for foreigners, as I later discovered. After partying all night , we returned to the National Hotel during the curfew at 4.00 am.

Of course, at this early stage in our relationship I spoke no Russian and our time together was punctuated by 'phone calls to her, at the end of which she would repeatedly say '*Yatojee*' to the caller. It was only later that I found out that the translation is 'Darling, I love you.' She was either talking to her boyfriend, I concluded, or if she was a spy, to her contact at a Ministry.

When I returned to London we kept up a correspondence for a time but, as with most 'holiday romances', the letter-writing petered out and finally there was silence.

During our Russian visit, we were invited to the dacha (country house or cottage in Russia) of Dr Federov, the developer and creator of the world's first laser treatments for patients requiring corrective eye surgery. Having perfected his technique over the years, he was celebrated internationally for effective and low-cost laser treatment, well before any Western practitioner in the same field.

The invitation arose as a result of my earlier work as the head of Patents International Group, where we had access to refined polymers that were used later in soft lenses and were sold worldwide. The original lens technology had come from the Czech

Republic but they had been unable to introduce sterilization into their technology until the introduction of soft lens polymers. Dr Federov had heard of this work in the field and I was invited for an informal stay of several days.

Dr Federov was a munificent host who also took the trouble to show me his project development work. I was more than impressed and could scarcely believe what we saw. His lifestyle was equally impressive and he had been accorded all the trappings of success. His Zil limousine wafted him through the Moscow traffic on the central lanes reserved for high-ranking government officials. His estate included stabling, with loose boxes for his thoroughbred horses (although Federov had lost the use of one of his legs, he still rode). We learnt later that he had his own airplane and that a special ship was being equipped for him as a roving hospital so that he could operate abroad outside the Soviet Union.

The evening banquet had everyone's mouth watering; the table groaned under every kind of fresh fish imaginable, caviar and imported lobster. It could easily have competed with Harrods Food Hall for its diversity. The lavish helpings of delicious food were helped down by the best vodka that money could buy. The bedrooms to which we were led after dinner were beautifully decorated and equipped with all the luxurious amenities, including bathrooms that one would expect to find in the West in the home of a rich banker.

The finale to the evening's entertainment came at midnight with a discreet knock at the door by a beautiful female assistant to ask if we would like to join the other guests for a nightcap. The other members of my group were already asleep but I decided to venture forth and accepted the invitation. I was led downstairs to an enormous den in the basement of the house furnished with a well-stocked bar, comfortable couches and a full-size billiard table. One wall was covered by a vast movie screen on which a John Wayne western was being shown. Completing the decorations were five beautiful girls whose sole function was to tend to the wishes of the all-male guests. Needless to say, I was particularly struck by a beautiful blonde, with the body of a Raquel Welch in her prime. I was pleasantly surprised to find that she spoke excellent English and we continued chatting well into the early hours of the morning. Everyone else retired and, without hesitation, she followed me to my room and enquired whether I needed company. We hugged and enjoyed the evening together. The following morning I promised to write to her from London, which I did.

As well as being a superb host and certainly someone who merited the perks and status given to him by the grateful State, Dr Federov also richly deserved the respect and high esteem in which he was held by his colleagues worldwide in the field of medical science. I will never forget his sense of humour and the generous Russian hospitality of that memorable visit.

He subsequently entered politics and tried to promote his ideas in the Duma (the Russian Parliament). Later, while piloting his own airplane at the age of 66, he died tragically when a bird flew into the engine and the plane crashed. He was accorded full honours at his State funeral. To this day there is no news of what happened to his hospital ship project, although the village he built for his personnel in the grounds of his dacha still stands. There, he had tried to teach his ideas for a better life while contributing to his ventures in the medical field.

My second brief visit to Russia at the invitation of the Russian Publishers' Association in the autumn of 1990, which I have already described, was for the sole purpose of clinching arrangements for a strong delegation of Russian publishing houses to attend the *Salon International du Livre* in Paris. By then the atmosphere in business and, indeed, in the streets of Moscow had changed dramatically after more than four years of *perestroika* policies under Mikhail Gorbachev, now President and an acknowledged world statesmen.

Looking back in perspective on that period, it is clear that for Russians the end of the 20th century was a story of lost dreams and lost promises. Prior to Gorbachev, the peoples of Eastern Europe were working out their drab and restricted daily lives while dreaming of breaking free from the political chains of total-itarian regimes. Although more cynical perhaps – after 70 years of the communist regime – about the benefits of adopting Western ways of life and Western institutions than the populations of the satellite Soviet states, patriotic Russians too dreamed of a better world. A world of real opportunities for the individual, a world in which they could explore and be creative. Because human beings are addicted to challenge, they play out their aspirations in the mind's eye and pictured themselves conquering new worlds, experiencing new emotions and building their dream castles.

And then came *perestroika*. For a few years, Russians were ecstatic with their perceived new freedom. In Moscow, the queues of citizens eager to eat at the newly opened MacDonalds wound round Derzhinsky Square; the 1990 Olympics attracted world media attention and an influx of foreign visitors; even high-ranking KGB officers appeared on TV chat shows; surely, this was Russia opening up to the outside world? Muscovites were flying; they were starting to live the dream. After the spring fever of *per-estroika*, could the summer of emerging democracy be far behind?

However, the euphoria was short-lived. All too soon they real-ized that the fetters that had limited their economic freedom for so many years remained. The political restraints were still there and had never been removed. What they had falsely taken as freedom was coming back to haunt them. All but a few remained chained to a world of economic failure.

What made matters even worse for ordinary Russians was that while before they had been able to dream, now they had lost the ability to perpetuate the dream. With their dreams destroyed, there was no bright sky at the end of their tunnel. Restricted by corruption and political games at all levels of authority and suffering from the result of disastrous economic policies, they now had to face a no-money world too. They could sense with their own senses and see with their own eyes that the world they had been yearning for existed, but they were still outsiders. That world was out of reach for them. Inevitably, they grew bitter and disillusioned. People without dreams are like birds without wings. You can take somebody's money, you can even deny people's freedom, but, by taking their dreams away, a whole generation was sentenced to live their lives as bodies without motivation.

It is difficult to survive in such a world of disillusionment and, being confused, Russians forgot how to believe in their own selves, in their ability to survive and how to search for their lost dreams. But that soon changed.

By the time I returned to Moscow for my third visit towards the end of 1990, at the invitation of the Director of Exhibitions of the Moscow Book Fair, Nikolai Ousianikov, disillusion had begun to set in. Although Gorbachev was still in power and had become a popular figure on the world stage, he was becoming less popular at home. There was little change in the standard of living for most Russians and the dream was starting to fade.

Nevertheless, the invitation to take on and improve the Moscow Book Fair as foreign co-managers of the September 1991 event was irresistible. Although the timing was short, the opportunity to step in and assist in the marketing of the primary Book Fair in Eastern Europe would be a vindication of much that we had tried to do through *European Bookseller* and at the *Salon International du Livre* I must admit that the prospective irritation factor for the Western publishing establishments, particularly the French, in being upstaged by the person whom they had thought to have squashed in Paris played its part in my decision to accept the challenge.

I signed the contract for the Moscow Book Fair and, with some of my old team, worked hard in London on my end of the deal.

We promoted Western involvement at the Book Fair, produced the catalogues and published a special edition of *European Bookseller*, featuring Russian publishers and their authors. The front cover of the issue carried the headline 'Lift-off for a Pluralist Soviet Publishing Industry' and included a review of Raisa Gorbachev's book *I Hope: Reminiscences and Reflections*, published by HarperCollins that September. The leading article in the Russian section of the issue was provided by Marat Shishigin, writing on the changing scene of Russian publishing and inviting foreign publishers to Moscow. All the leading Russian publishing houses were featured in the issue, together with prominent publishers from the Commonwealth of Independent States (CIS) such as Belarus, Kazakhstan and the Urals.

In the same issue, Jonathan Reuvid published his attack on the Frankfurt Book Fair under the heading 'Achtung Dinosaur', arguing that smaller regional book fairs were more efficient and that the introduction of sophisticated information technology would make Frankfurt's mega-role as the premier International Rights Fair redundant.

In the interval of preparation for Moscow, we continued to move ahead on our other fronts. The 1st Prague International Book Fair in May was an outstanding success. During its three-day run, nearly 40,000 visited the Exhibition at the Palace of Culture, which featured more than 200 exhibitors from some of the biggest names in international publishing to the smaller, independent Czech and Slovak publishers. Czechoslovakia's largest importer and wholesaler of books reported book purchases of over US$2 million at its stand alone. Ferdinand Mount, Editor of the *Times Literary Supplement,* attended the show and commented 'Now is the precise moment for European culture to meet and write in the common cause of literature. Prague is central to that aim.'

The Prague Writers' Festival was held at the Palffy Palace and attended by a packed audience of 500. The theme of the meeting was 'Wedding Preparations in the Country: the Divorce of Politics and Culture', which reflected precisely the mood of the time. The centrepiece of the Festival was the annual George Theiner Translation Prize, honouring the memory of the distinguished Czech translator and editor. The prize was awarded to the Czech poet Miroslav Horub by Michael March, as Director of the Writers' Festival on behalf of *European Bookseller*. At the close of the Fair, the 2nd Prague International Book Fair was announced for 14–17 May 1992.

We also took responsibility, on behalf of Western publishers, of managing the logistics for the delivery of books to the Moscow show, which was to be held in the ageing VDNK Exhibition Centre where the Book Fair and other cultural events were held. Although we had only just over six months to market the Moscow Book Fair and complete all these arrangements, I felt that we had done a good job. I was confident of success as I boarded the plane for Moscow again on the eve of the fair at the end of August 1991.

I was met at Moscow Airport by Edouard , who had been my collaborator with Mikhail in cajoling and herding the Russian delegation of publishers to the *Salon International du Livre* in Paris. and had been eager to co-operate with the Moscow Book Fair, which they regarded as unfinished business. During the preparation period, he had undertaken the local liaison with the Moscow Book Fair. Accompanied by Edouard's girlfriend and her female friend Katya, who was there to make up a foursome, I was driven to the Belgrade Hotel in the city centre (to aid confusion, there were two Belgrade Hotels in Moscow at that time: Belgrade No1 and Belgrade No2).

The check-in took an astonishing one and a half hours. As I watched the receptionist copy my passport by hand, I assumed that the staff were just being incompetent, but in fact there were two reasons why the process was so slow. In the first place, there was no photocopier, but, more importantly, Edouard had arranged for me to pay in roubles. Local currency payment reduced the cost significantly but took much longer to process. The four of us – myself, Edouard, his girlfriend and the girlfriend's girlfriend Katya went for a drink at the bar and I then retired to my room. By now, I was tired from my journey and rather uneasy at being in a strange country without any of my own staff. As always in a new hotel room when travelling, I turned on the television and soon dropped off to sleep.

I awoke some time later to see the Russian Minister of Culture on the TV screen holding a book. My first reaction was that this was free publicity for the Book Fair and I telephoned Edouard to tell him the good news. 'No, *durak* (stupid),' Edouard rebuked me. On the contrary, the news was bad. Something had happened to the government and the Minister was announcing that the Moscow Book Fair was cancelled. At that moment, there was a knock at the door and, when I opened it, there stood Katya. I had no idea how she had got past the formidable *babushkas*, the head-scarved old ladies on the landing of each floor whom I had encountered on my first visit, who still acted as guards and informants on the more clandestine activities of the guests.

That was how Katya came into my life. She was an exceptionally beautiful and striking girl – especially her skin – and, as I soon discovered, totally uninhibited. I offered her a drink that first evening and she explained that she could not stay long because she had to beat the curfew and must leave by 11.00 pm. Before she left, Katya told me directly in her attractive broken English that she would like to get to know me. She gave me her telephone number and told me that the best times to call would be before 8.00 am or after 11.00 pm, but not too late. She then startled me by giving me a kiss and startled me again by asking for US$10. I didn't understand at the time why she wanted the money, but found out later that it was to bribe the *babushka* guarding my floor of the hotel, so that she could get out of the hotel without any problems.

The following morning I arose early, first to call Katya before 8.00 am to make a date for that evening and then to investigate the threatened cancellation of the Moscow Book Fair. Assuming wrongly that Katya and I had made love the night before, the *babushka* gave me a big smile when I left my room – a pleasant change from her normal grim and disapproving expression. For my part, I still couldn't work out why someone like Katya would want to see someone like me.

My first port of call that morning was the Offices of the Book Fair, where the full extent of the political upheaval became apparent. Overnight, a faction of hard-line old school communists, led by Gaspulatov, Speaker of the Russian Parliament, and the Chief of the Russian Air Force ('Rushkoi'), who were unhappy with his Presidency had attempted a coup to overthrow Gorbachev. The coup leaders took possession of the White House where Russia's Parliament – the Duma – was located and tried to persuade a majority of Duma members to support them. In the few days that followed, Boris Yeltsin – a former ally – who had also been one of Mikhail Gorbachev's most persistent public critics, now took a leading role in the struggle for power. It was clear that the conspirators would fail without the support of the army, to which Yeltsin appealed successfully. Tanks were drawn up in front of and encircling the White House. The rest, as they say, is history. In a dramatic moment, Yeltsin climbed on top of a tank and harangued the crowd assembled outside and the delegates closeted inside. He admonished them not to destroy the progress of the *perestroika* years but to build on the period's successes and demanded in the name of the Russian people that the 'reactionaries' surrender. This grand gesture in the mould of archetypal revolutionary heroes was lovingly recorded by the world's media and replayed again and again on Russian television, where it appealed strongly to all Russians. After a few tank salvoes were fired at the White House, inflicting superficial damage to the façade, the coup leaders gave up and that crisis was over. Eight months later, there was a second crisis while Gorbachev and his family were on holiday at their dacha on the Black Sea. They were placed under arrest. At Yeltsin's insistence, Gorbachev was released and brought back to Moscow as President for a short time but it was clear that power had passed to Yeltsin. The latter was soon afterwards elected President of Russia, effectively sidelining Gorbachev by engineering the dissolution of the USSR. The Presidency of the Soviet Union subsequently ceased to exist.

However, at the time, none of these counter-coup actions, nor the subsequent outcome, helped me or the Moscow Book Fair exhibitors. On the morning after the coup, I was told that there was 'no way' that the Moscow Book Fair could go ahead because there was no administration in place; the Director General of the Book Fair had disappeared, leaving his staff stranded. I called the British Embassy to find a contact in the Yeltsin faction. I told the contact I was given that the cancellation of the Moscow Book Fair would reflect very badly on Russia and said that I needed permission to hold it. Within 24 hours of my call, while Boris Yeltsin was atop his tank, the contact within his group called me back to say that it was not safe for people to go on the streets and the fair must be cancelled because neither visitors nor exhibitors could be protected. I now had to confront the difficult situation of telling the exhibitors that the Moscow Book Fair was not going to happen and that they should prepare to go home.

The situation was chaotic. Pandemonium at the airport stopped some exhibitors from leaving; others had to stay because they had fixed period tickets. The Moscow Book Fair staff were pleased that I stayed on because I could contact the western exhibitors in their hotels to explain to them why the show was cancelled. My own position was calamitous as I stood to lose all my investment in the project. After the frustration of the Paris Book Fair boycott, I had managed to persuade potential exhibitors to come to Moscow instead. Now I was facing the embarrassing and even more frustrating task of telling the people to whom I had sold space in the Moscow Book Fair that it, too, had aborted. In a first attempt to contain the losses, I asked the management of the VDNK centre to postpone the Book Fair to the following year. 'Not possible,' I was told, because the Book Fair was held every two years, 'according to the State Five-Year Plan.' Since there was no longer the same communist government or a five-year plan, the logic seemed shaky, but there was no point in arguing.

My next attempt to save something from the ashes of defeat was to offer exhibitors a credit against future Moscow Book Fairs as compensation in lieu of refunds. Some of the smaller publishers who could least afford it accepted. Perversely, the larger exhibitors with government-backed stands wanted a full refund. While the British were sympathetic and helpful, the French and Germans, reflecting their opposition to the Paris *Salon International du Livre*, were not. Predictably, they declared their intention of having future Moscow Book Fairs controlled by the Frankfurt Book Fair.

Thus, the lines for future battles were drawn between my company and the Russians on one side, and the Germans and various governments on the other.

There were other compensations for me in staying on. My blossoming friendship with Katya in the hectic days that followed was an effective salve to the disappointment of the Moscow Book Fair cancellation. Our first date was not altogether a success. I had arranged to meet her for a drink in the Belgrade Hotel at 7.00 pm. I should have guessed that I would be stuck in the VDNK office trying to calm the demands of disaffected exhibitors and, in those days when we still existed without mobile 'phones, I was unable to reach her. Having missed the date, I finally reached the restaurant where we had chosen to dine at 9.00 pm. Katya was understandably annoyed, thinking that I had stood her up deliberately. Most of the rest of that evening was spent in explanations and soothing ruffled feathers.

The next time we met, Katya explained that she could not return to the hotel with me 'because they wouldn't let her in and I would have to come to her apartment.' That was the beginning of our affair. As our relationship developed, Katya took me to all the tourist sites in Moscow and I felt as if I was on my honeymoon. At a time when my business was crashing about my ears, I found that Katya was acting as a positive force to balance out the negative impact of my work. She also helped me with my more difficult calls to exhibitors, adding a Russian dimension to explanations as to why the fair had been cancelled.

One of the problems was that we had no car, which had an effect on our relationship as it restricted our movements, and using taxis could be difficult. I remember one occasion in particular when I was staying overnight at Katya's apartment in the Moscow suburbs and woke early worrying about work. I decided that I had to get back to the hotel and set out on foot. At that time, it was commonplace to stop cars and ask for a lift, but I was out of luck that chilly dawn as there was little traffic. Finally, I was able to flag down an ambulance that delivered me safely to the hotel.

I had realised soon after my arrival that I had little understanding of how Russians thought and reacted in the rapidly changing environment. My relationship with Katya and growing friendship with Edouard, coupled with the pressure of events, provided the learning curve for me to shed my rookie status rapidly.

I learned that Russians are not people who will show or exhibit their true emotions, but that deep inside they are very vulnerable. This fact explains much of their behavioural strangeness. Most Westerners never try to understand them. Russians are not open and will never express feelings, even when it comes to a simple business communication. At the same time, they pay great attention to details and judge you according to your behaviour, manners and thoughts. I found out that they never start any brainstorming discussions with new ideas, even if they have them. They will expect you to be the first to start. It is like a game, but a silent one, which most foreign businesspeople never understand they are playing. Strangely, Russians are not usually able to express any feeling of respect or affection. Their thought processes are guided much more by cold logic than those of many other nationalities.

People should not be offended, or even upset, by this apparent coldness. I soon realised that their behavioural pattern is a reflection of the way they are created and that it is entirely normal. Russians have different codes of morality and different values. Russians are as naughty and as full of life as anyone else. The difference is that they do not like talking or boasting about their private lives. For example, I have noticed that neither men nor women mention their '*amours*'. This is not because they do not have any or are not excited about them; they are taken simply as a part of everyday life and there is nothing to discuss or to show off about. It is also noticeable that they take their affairs very, very seriously and pay great attention to one another, something of which I think they are also very proud. I have sometimes found it very difficult to understand Russians because of their almost total lack of communication skills. That is why many people in many cases find them rude, or even abusive. I found them to be 'honest' and, on the contrary, the foreigners' reaction to be rude.

Thanks to Katya's efforts in helping to deal with frustrated foreign publishers, I was developing a good rapport with the VDNK management team. With the idea of postponing the Moscow Book Fair by a year being firmly rejected, talks moved on to what else could be staged in the VDNK in the odd year between Book Fairs. After several late night brainstorming sessions, the suggestions that predominated among the ideas that were put forward were an international plastics and packaging exhibition or other industrial themes. My brother Roddy insisted that a bigger theme – such as an international motor show – was preferable, to justify the higher risk factor at that time of going into a new market such as Russia. We decided that other major exhibition themes to follow, if we were successful, would include oil and gas and tele-communications. Energy Exhibitions were activities in which I had some experience – mostly successful – from Nigeria to China. Like China, the logic for an automobile show in Russia was simply that so few people actually owned them and that the high level of curiosity would ensure a good attendance. From the auto manu-facturers' point of view, Russia was a key emerging market, where business opportunities were opening up following the détente with the West forged by Presidents Ronald Reagan and Mikhail Gorbachev through their campfire diplomacy in Iceland.

And so, the idea of the Moscow International Motor Show 1992 was born. It was time to take stock of my situation. After successive Book Fair disasters in Paris and now Moscow, my finances were suffering second degree burns from the 'Bonfire of my Book Trade Vanities' but I did not feel mortally wounded. As always, I was determined not to be beaten and a Moscow Motor Show offered more than a beacon of hope. Once again in my rollercoaster career, as one door closed, another had opened.

Chapter 5

The Moscow Motor Shows

Back in London, before committing irrevocably to organizing the International Motor Show in Moscow, I had to re-evaluate where I was going. The unexpected International Book Fair failure in Paris and then the cancellation in Moscow in the space of eight months had taken their toll. My spirits, which had been sustained in Moscow, were now at a low ebb and I needed to restore my self-confidence.

Really, there were two issues to confront. Although the first and most pressing was the Moscow Motor Show, I also had to decide whether or not to continue developing book fairs in the CEE.

The main issue involved an act of faith rather than cold logic. If I was to accept the new challenge in Moscow, I would have to commit more of my financial resources and there was no guarantee of a successful outcome. On the upside were the strong impression that Russia was on the verge of exploding into an era of entrepreneurship – much as China had done after 1978, the personal goodwill that I had forged in Moscow and my confidence in the ability and reliability of my new Russian friends. On the downside were the extreme difficulties that all Western companies were experiencing at that time in doing profitable business with Russia or gaining an investment foothold; and my own personal past experience of entering China too soon in the early stages of its long march to a market economy. On balance, I decided that the opportunities were greater than the threats and that my past experience of the pitfalls of trade show and trade centre development in China, London and Paris would stand me in good stead for avoiding any Russian bear-traps that I might encounter. As my self-confidence revived, I suppose that the deciding factor in signing up finally to the Moscow Motor Show was the innate spirit of adventure that had brought me so far. I had snow on my boots from my first Russian winter but was disinclined to emulate Napoleon by retreating from Moscow.

The decision to continue with book fair development was less controversial. I decided to capitalize on the success of the 1st Prague International Book Fair and Writers' Festival, now firmly scheduled for its second year, by repeating the formula first in Bucharest in June 1992 and then in Sofia, Bulgaria, and hopefully Budapest and Warsaw. The Prague model of a Writers' Festival as the intellectual mortar for the construction of a successful international book fair seemed appropriate for the whole region.

In the event, the second Prague International Book Fair had a rocky ride when the Frankfurt Book Fair and the French Syndicat National de l'Edition intervened again to persuade the Minister of Culture to displace us on the grounds that I had been 'boycotted in France' and had 'failed' in Russia. It was rumoured that the Minister's wife had been paid an advance by a German publisher to publish a book which she intended to write as an inducement to cancel our arrangement. We foiled the conspiracy by threatening legal proceedings against both the Minister and his wife. I had booked the space for a five-year tenure and, despite warnings from the Ministry of Culture, we went on with the second Book Fair with the backing of the Czech publishing house Zahranicni Literatura. Our book fair was again a great success. The Germans held their own fair a month later, but it was not a success, with only German publishers exhibiting. Subsequently, we reached an agreement to cede future Prague International Book Fairs to the Palace of Culture and the Frankfurt Book Fair in return for three years' tenure of a new Prague Language Fair and adequate compensation from the Palace of Culture.

I would never have given up on future Prague Book Fairs had it not been for investigations by the then Czech Government of Zahranicni Literatura's General Director, Frank Brecha, our supporter and sponsor. Trumped up charges against him as a previous sympathizer of Russia and communist movements led to his dismissal and arrest. Only when we relented were the charges dropped without any explanation and he was released. The direct intervention of President Havel was later cited as the reason. My friendship with Frank continued to grow over the years and later he was able to make an immense contribution to our expansion in Russia.

The *European Bookseller*, which had established my reputation as a credible partner in book fair organization, continued in its proven format through to the spring of 1992, when it celebrated its second birthday. By now, it had fulfilled its original purpose of opening up communications between Western publishing and the emergent writers and publishing houses of the CEE.

Planning an international motor exhibition in Moscow was not easy. Russia was in political turmoil, there were few staff at the VDNK Exhibition Centre and there was little more than six months' planning time available. I approached my brother Roddy, now retired, for his help. However, Roddy took the view that it would be impossible to organize the Motor Show with just six months' notice and declined the project. Nevertheless, Roddy and I did organize a conference on Investing in Czechoslovakia that year, which was a financial success, although some speakers failed to turn up and the rest were drunk.

I was committed to hiring the space at the VDNK Exhibition
Centre for the proposed International Motor Show the following
year (1992), and had to pay for it up front. Fortunately, Roddy
relented and agreed to step in as a partner. Two Russian partners,
Edouard and Nicolai were also added, increasing the management from one to four, with a 50/50 split between them and the
Shashoua brothers.

While I managed the logistics, Roddy handled the marketing.
Initially, Volvo and their would-be partners at that time, Renault,
committed to the show as they wished to be placed together. They
were swiftly followed by the Italians and then the British, led by
Rolls Royce, with German, Japanese and Detroit auto manufacturers bringing up the rear. In the end, 90 per cent of the major
auto manufacturers signed up for the show; only 10 per cent did
not, and this was simply because there was no exhibition space
left for them.

The administration and logistics of the Motor Show were as
much a nightmare as the selling of exhibition space. Although we
had spent nothing on advertising, as we would have done for a
Western Motor Show, the manufacturers expected good promotional exposure and service. Nor had they adjusted their mindsets
to the totally different circumstances in Russia. Despite all of this,
the opening of the 1st International Moscow Motor Show was
attended in force by the international press and TV news channels
curious to see how a people starved of cars for so many years
would respond. And, contrary to the misgivings of the exhibitors,
when the media interviewed the public attending the show, they
found that people were buying cars. In fact, most exhibitors
declared that, had they known what sort of a future market was
there in Russia, they would have signed up for the show even
sooner.

In essence, foreign auto manufacturers considered their participation in Moscow for the first time as a PR exercise to establish
their brand names for future sales in this giant new market. Ironically, on the opening day, almost all of the several hundred cars

on display were snapped up by local buyers. This created a logistical problem for PR staff manning their stands. As a result, they had to line up for hours in single file to get through to their headquarters by telephone; there was only one external telephone trunk line on site. Dramatically, they insisted that their export managers fly out immediately to Moscow with sales contract forms so as to complete the sale of the automobiles at the close of the show. They were anxious to avoid some local threats that they would not be allowed to leave Moscow without selling the cars on display.

Like every other business activity in which I have been involved, the Motor Show was peppered with incidents, both humorous and otherwise.

One prospective buyer showed interest in a bullet-proof car. 'Is this car bullet proof?' he asked. He was told that it was, whereupon he pulled out an automatic pistol and sprayed the side of the vehicle liberally with bullets. 'It is bullet-proof! he declared. 'I'll take two of them, but not this one because it is damaged!'

Another young Russian with his two assistants carrying cash-filled briefcases wanted to buy a Lamborghini Diablo on display in time for a date with a beautiful woman that night and was crestfallen to have to wait until the end of the show.

During the show, I was somewhat taken aback when I was approached by my two Russian partners to be told that they were taking over. I asked them about the profits share. 'Whose profits?' they replied, with success going to their heads. Instead of pursuing the discussion with them, I took myself off to the exhibition floor to see how well the show was doing and to ponder how I was going to break the news to Roddy that we would be displaced. Then it struck me that the bulk of the profits were coming from the international exhibitors whose paid-for participation Roddy had sold and negotiated, not from the Russian exhibitors. Being pushed out by our Russian partners meant that Roddy and I would take the lion's share of the profits rather than the 50 per cent share that we would have received as partners.

The success of the show was beyond our Russian 'partners' wildest dreams and thrust them into the limelight. Being featured personally on virtually all the TV networks and in Russian magazines was something neither one could never have imagined and it went to their heads. Roddy and I deliberately ignored the media, preferring a low profile in those unsettled times.

In addition to the old VDNK Exhibition Centre, Moscow also had a newer 100,000 square-metre facility, the Krasnaya Presnya Expo-Centre, controlled by the Russian Chamber of Commerce. To move the Motor Show from the old VDNK, which was largely for cultural events, to the new ExpoCentre, normally used for commercial exhibitions, seemed eminently sensible, especially to the Expo officials who paid Edouard a visit. You will have some impression of the VDNK's limitations if you have ever seen the movie *The Russia House*, starring Sean Connery as a minor British publisher who becomes involved in espionage. Incidentally, the Book Fair sequences shot on location in the VDNK include a scene in which Edouard – ever the extrovert self-publicist – was allocated a one-liner greeting to Sean Connery and Michelle Pfeiffer.

Edouard needed little persuasion to move 'his' Motor Show for the next year but when he arrived at the new ExpoCentre to negotiate, just a month after the first Motor Show had ended, he was in for a shock. First, he was told that space at the shiny new ExpoCentre would cost more than double that at the tired old VDNK. This information was not too surprising, but what followed was a hammer blow. The ExpoCentre management informed Edouard that they had been planning a Motor Show of their own and, accordingly, ExpoCentre would be running the Motor Show, not him, from now on. Just to rub salt into Edouard's wounds and humiliate him thoroughly, the Expo managers hinted that they could be persuaded to take him on as a salesman for the show.

Next, in order to bolster their claim, the ExpoCentre launched a newspaper campaign against Edouard. The German auto manufacturers joined forces with the ExpoCentre to participate in the show. The luckless Edouard found himself completely out of his depth and returned to us, asking to be taken back.

Without any delay, Roddy went back to the major international motor manufacturers to convince them that they should book their exhibition space for next year at the VDNK. The German auto manufacturers tried to put us off, but all the other major international manufacturers signed up with us for 1993. A month and a half later, all the auto manufacturers received a letter from the ExpoCentre informing them that their show was the official one because it was backed not only by the Russian Government but also by the International Association of Motor Manufacturers (OICA).

At this stage, Roddy and I were almost ready to throw in the towel and concede defeat. Then we heard that the Russian fiscal police were ready to raid the Moscow offices that we had taken over from Edouard. This meant that ExpoCentre were resorting to dirty tricks in an attempt not only to take over the Motor Show but also to ruin Edouard and his successors personally. This action stiffened our resolve, having the opposite effect to that intended. Immediately, we wrote to the major auto manufacturers saying that they could go to ExpoCentre if they paid the confirmed booking fees that were due to our ITE Group, as it was the rightful contracted exhibition. In return, we asked them to wait for two months – to give us some breathing space – so that if we did put on the Motor Show they would not have to pay their fees twice. Having bought time, both Edouard and I went to the top, the office of the Russian Prime Minister. At the same time, Edouard decided to join our Group as General Director of the Moscow office.

My choice of tactics was guided by my rapidly growing understanding of the Russian character. I knew that if I demanded my rights from officials or politicians, we would be ignored and possibly prosecuted. A legalistic approach might have worked in the West, but definitely not here in Russia. Instead, we went to the Prime Minister's office and asked for his help. That made all the difference. The OICA headquarters in Paris was controlled by an official from Daimler-Benz as Secretary General; therefore, we did not expect the OICA to support our case. The Russian Prime Minister adopted an oblique approach, by writing to the Russian Ambassador in Paris who, in turn, wrote to the secretary of the OICA advising him that the dispute was between the ExpoCentre and the VDNK. Therefore, the OICA was instructed, it should not become involved and the auto manufacturers should be free to make their own choice. Edouard was given the satisfaction of delivering the ambassador's letter by hand to the secretary general. On receiving the letter from Edouard, the secretary general flew into a rage, flung the letter to the floor, questioning whether or not it was genuine and stated that he did not care about either ambassadors or Russia and would not listen to any arguments. This was hardly a victory for diplomacy, but the letter served its purpose.

Three months before our second Motor Show at the VDNK, all the major international manufacturers, except the Germans, had paid their fees to ITE Group in London. We had promised our exhibitors that the VDNK show would have not only more exhibitors but also a higher attendance because it was a proven success – now in its second year – and would naturally receive all the publicity. And so it proved. While the VDNK show included most of the world's auto manufacturers, only the Germans and the Russians exhibited at the ExpoCentre Motor Show. The ExpoCentre people had missed the basic point that the World's media would not bother coming to a second motor show when the already proven successful event in the same city had closed. Following our success, the ExpoCentre vowed to make sure that there would be no space available for us at the VDNK or anywhere else in Russia in future years. This situation was finally resolved three months later to everyone's satisfaction.

★

The second Moscow Motor Show, like the first, involved a crop of humorous, bizarre and threatening incidents. We had 3,000 T-shirts printed with the words 'International Motor Show' in blue on a white background to be handed out as promotional give-aways. At the Press Preview for the opening, we found that 1,000 T-shirts had suddenly disappeared – they were sold to visitors outside the building. Edouard explained that in Russia nothing was given away free. Everything should be exchanged or bartered and he had exchanged the T-shits for the bonuses due to the firemen and security staff who had worked round the clock to ensure the success of the show. True to form, Edouard held back another 500 T-shirts, which he distributed personally to almost every pretty girl whom he encountered in the hope of filling his address book with potential conquests.

The good quality carpeting that the stand constructor had supplied to cover the holes in the surface of the old exhibition centre floor disappeared almost as quickly as it was laid on the ground. Local exhibitors and visitors alike, having felt the quality of the carpets, rushed out to buy shears and helped themselves. They rolled up sections of carpet and carried them on their backs to their cars. Over 4,000 square metres of the 6,000 square metres of carpet laid were removed in this way, leaving behind an expo floor with holes that resembled Swiss cheese.

All was not harmony among the exhibitors. Those who were displaying their products on the balcony level, when washing their cars, paid no regard to those exhibitors below who had worked hard to wax their cars to perfection, only to have them showered with dirty water from above.

The old VDNK building was the cause of another threat to exhibitors when we instructed the ten *babushkas* – who were the exhibition's cleaning ladies – to wash its glass windows, which had not been cleaned for years. They took pails of water outside and threw the contents at the glass walls, ignoring the fact that some of the windows were open. Consequently, water filtered through on to the shiny exhibits. The outside was now clean, but to the detriment of the cars displayed inside.

There were also dramatic confrontations with some of those who attended the Motor Show. A visit from 'the heavies' included a request to purchase all the cars off the stands at the end of the show. My staff and I told them that we did not own the cars and so, regretfully, could not give them away although they were more than welcome to make their requests to our exhibitors direct. However, I could give the heavies a useful tip. 'Try the Germans at the ExpoCentre; they are the ones with plenty of money and are certain to give a few cars away!' I was pleased to extend this courtesy to our competitor.

Meanwhile, Edouard was very happy at the success of the toy, remote-controlled motor cars, which he was offering for sale to the public at affordable prices. While their children bought the toy cars in quantity, their parents gazed in wonder at the latest models of real automobiles on display at prices within the reach of only the very few. You might say that it was an omen of today's Russian automotive market. In 2006, Russia accounted for more luxury cars than all of Europe combined and the Russian automotive market is still increasing at an annual rate of 25 per cent in 2007.

When the competing ExpoCentre Motor Show – named 'Auto Salon'– came to an end, Edouard and I decided to pay a visit to the end-of-show drinks party as uninvited guests. At first, we were unable to spot the organizers at the reception. Then Edouard noticed that a table was blocking the doors to the banqueting room. We scrambled under the table and gained entry to the banqueting room, the inner sanctum where, lo and behold, we found the organizers hobnobbing with generals and politicians. Seizing the moment and a glass of champagne, I bounced straight up to the director of the ExpoCentre, introduced myself, and toasted the success of the ExpoCentre Auto Salon. While most of the room raised their glasses in response, three dissenting voices from the Russian OICA members rang out. Edouard translated for me. 'Shit,' they said 'it's the worst organized show we have ever been to.'

To his great credit, the ExpoCentre director recognized the validity of his critics' complaints. We suggested to him that, in spite of past conflicts, we should set aside our differences and join forces to organize the 3rd Motor Show at ExpoCentre. The Russian OICA members agreed to sponsor and to be a partner in our future Motor Shows. ExpoCentre then conceded and awarded us a five-year lease. We were back in business with an assured future for a highly profitable annual Motor Trade Show. This accord also laid the foundation for the rapid rise of the ITE Group in Russia.

Chapter 6

Natasha – The Rise of a New Russian Woman

'The essence of Russia is held in the palm of a Russian woman's hand'.

Formerly, during the long period of the communist regime, women in Russia led a subservient existence. Their aspirations and ambitions to build a career and life for themselves were ruthlessly suppressed. Typically, a girl born and brought up in one region or city would be allocated to a specific factory when she reached working age.

The most that an attractive girl could hope for – if her family had connections within the Party to a local official or factory manager – was to work for him, which usually entailed sleeping with him too. There was little prospect of advancement except under her boss within the same office or factory and no hope of moving job to another local work unit. Jobs were for life with an apartment allocated to the employee.

There were no foreign firms or private companies in Russia that she could hope to work for. Nor was there any hope of moving to another city or region.

All passports, without which movement was in any case impossible, showed both address and occupation; any woman found elsewhere was likely to be arrested, returned and punished.

Prior to 1992, life for Russian women must have seemed 'less complex' than for Western women. Less distracted by modern conveniences, they had a simple outlook on life. Basically, they looked for a man who would 'provide life's essentials' and they would be faithful in return.

Hope for the intelligent and resourceful of something better returned only when foreign companies or foreign-invested joint ventures opened offices in Russia. Here, at last, was an opportunity for those women with an entrepreneurial spirit to break free from their shackles by seeking employment with foreign firms.

In recent years, the media has been full of stories of the rise and, in some cases fall, of Russia's male oligarchs. It is time now to pay tribute to the remarkable generation of thousands of talented young Russian women brought up in the pre-*perestroika* period who seized their opportunities for fame and fortune in the free-wheeling turbulent times of Boris Yeltsin's presidency in the 1990s, in order to claw their way to the top.

One of these formidable and attractive young ladies was my dear friend Natasha. This is her tale.

I first met Natasha at the opening of the 2nd Moscow Motor Show when the band was playing and she and her girlfriend were trying to obtain tickets to the VIP section. I agreed to provide entry on the assumption that she was meeting one of the VIPs who had invited her and, of course, I didn't want to upset him. I took her name and telephone number and invited her as my guest to the receptions that followed. She was beautiful and certainly a trophy to be seen with among the models at the Motor Show. I dissuaded her from applying for a modelling job herself at the show, which would have wasted her career opportunities. She was not only beautiful but bright and certainly ambitious. I promised to introduce her to some friends in the industry who could make better use of her talents.

Natasha was grateful for my advice and patience in helping her and, after a couple of dates, invited me over for dinner to meet her family. It was at this modest dinner in her 50 square metre one-and-a-half-room apartment that I met her daughter and mother. Her father was deceased and she and her mother were doing all they could to support themselves. The mother, having worked most of her life, had saved and paid for Natasha's education and she had just finished her university degree. Her mother praised me for my advice, as she was strongly against her daughter becoming a model with no future. Against this backdrop, our affair blossomed and flourished and I took a real interest in helping her to get started in the business world.

It wasn't long into her relationship with me that Natasha became aware of her 'inadequacies'. She was beautiful but needed to dress better and her English was poor. At times, when we went out among sophisticated company, I felt that I had to 'hide' her. However, unlike many of her contemporaries, Natasha was not content to look back to the period when women were effectively prisoners of the State. Instead, she looked forwards and saw in me a means to an end in making more of herself. Natasha invested in herself in order to push herself ahead, by buying good quality Western clothes and make-up, and by learning English.

Her investment soon paid off. Now she looked good, spoke English well, felt confident and had updated her computer skills. With these assets, her next step to independence was to find a job with a joint venture company. The first company that she worked for was a partnership of the international accountancy firm Coopers & Lybrand, where she was appointed as Personal Assistant (PA) to a senior director of the Moscow office. Beautifully dressed and Western in appearance, she was deliberately very attentive, worked long hours, took work home at the weekends and learned the ways in which she could best help her director. Over a period of time, she became more and more *au fait* with the intricacies of the job, while her boss became more and more dependent on her and increasingly took her to business meetings.

The managing director also took Natasha on trips abroad. Gaining an insight into life outside Russia fascinated her even more and increased her eagerness to learn. By working for a joint venture, Natasha could earn (in roubles) between US$1,000–1,500 per month, compared to the average salary of around US$200 a month of a secretary working for a Russian company in the early 1990s.

Inevitably, as her director became more dependent on her, he became closer to her. Natasha did not really want a personal relationship with him but, because she also had to look after her daughter from an earlier marriage and her elderly mother, she knew that she could not afford to lose her enhanced salary. Although the director was married, Natasha agreed to start an affair with him and the 'perks' of the relationship helped her to look after her family.

Although Natasha already had a degree in Law, she asked her superiors if she could study for accountancy qualifications in order to further her career in the firm. Selfishly, he told her that she would never be able to do that, not because of any lack of innate ability but because he did not want to lose such an invaluable PA. Not only was Natasha very useful to him; he also loved her and did not want to lose her personal company.

Nevertheless, one of the partners in the company did encourage her to study accountancy and also took her to social functions where she met the 'New Rich' of Moscow society and 'learnt the ropes' of mixing with Russian plutocrats. By now, her director was on a roll. The Moscow office had expanded from 30 to over 200 accountants and his affair with Natasha had not hindered but was in fact actively helping his career. Natasha's situation was less satisfactory. After two years, she was still a PA and, despite her reasonably high salary, she decided it was time to move on. A further factor was the growing jealousy of the director, who did not appreciate the partner's interest in Natasha, and whom she felt might be plotting to get rid of her.

One of the accountancy practice's clients was a 'new' Russian company of motorcar dealers that had started life as a small repair shop and had grown into an automobile distribution agency with a US$60-million turnover. Boris, the Chairman of the company, was very impressed with Natasha's efficiency and offered to double her salary and give her a company car if she would agree to become his office manager. This was an offer that could not be refused. After 18 months with her new employer, Natasha had gained sufficient experience to run the company whenever the chairman was away on business.

The company's clients were particularly impressed by the beautiful and well-organized Natasha, whose efficiency contrasted sharply with the incompetence and inefficiency they encountered daily in their other dealings. She also managed to look after the clients to their satisfaction while maintaining a respectable distance. Natasha had become a real asset to the company, as she had previously to the Coopers & Lybrand partnership. The chairman – a married man aged 30 with three children, a Range Rover and a Mercedes Benz 600 to look after – felt that the only way to keep Natasha was to have an affair with her.

His chance came when he invited Natasha to fly to a dealers' convention with him in Antalya, Turkey. On their second night there, Natasha received a package from him delivered to her room. It contained a fabulous necklace, bracelet and earrings set, which cost US$25,000. Boris had no credit card; so she realised that he must have taken the risk of carrying that amount of cash just to buy her a gift. She found out the value of the jewels almost immediately when Boris followed up the dispatch of his present with a visit to her hotel room. In a rather brusque fashion he told her that he cared for her and that – by the way he had paid

US$25,000! Not exactly romantic, but whereas previously she had thought that he was tough and exploitative; now she realized that he had a more caring side. The fact that he had taken the risk, and that he genuinely seemed to care, persuaded Natasha to take a chance on him.

Back in Moscow, Natasha and Boris continued to see each other. From time to time, he showered her with gifts but, more importantly, he bought her a US$150,000 apartment, complete with two bedrooms and bathroom. Previously, she had been living in a cramped studio flat. Now her mother could sleep in her own room and Natasha could sleep with her daughter in the other bedroom. The kitchen was big enough to accommodate and serve as a dining room and they all shared the living room. She could also rent out her old apartment and receive an increasing rent.

The one drawback to these arrangements was that Boris had a hold over her now, because the apartment was held in their joint names. If anything went wrong with the affair, Natasha was only half-owner. Contentment was short-lived. Things did start going wrong – Boris's wife found out about Natasha. Both he and his wife started to drink heavily. Natasha could see that if their affair continued – and he carried on drinking heavily – the business would collapse and, because the business was his life, his family would be destroyed. Natasha decided that she could not be responsible for such an outcome and that she had to leave. Natasha told Boris that she could not see him any more and she wanted to start up in business on her own. He took it very badly but realised that he could not leave his wife and children. Natasha repaid Boris over three years for his share of the apartment and they remained good friends.

The car dealership sold only expensive automobiles, and Natasha started to date one of its wealthiest clients, who was in the oil and gas business. After going out with him for a month, Natasha asked her date if he would help her to start up in business as a travel agency. He agreed to invest and lend her about US$500,000 to set up an office, hire a staff of two assistants and have sufficient credit to buy tickets (as an unaccredited travel agent she had to pay in cash for them up front) before selling them on to customers. In the first instance, she set up as the back office to a larger travel agency so that she could learn the business. Her margins were low and the work was not glamorous but she was happy because, finally, she owned her own business. However, by a stroke of fate, her entry into the travel business resulted in our meeting again.

The travel agency business was buoyant. After the break-up of the state-controlled Intourist, some 5,000 privately-run agencies had sprung up in a matter of only 12 months. In the same period, as privatization became the watchword in Russia, around 600 banks has set up shop but without the sort of basic regulation to which Western banks have to conform and regardless of whether or not they had adequate capital. Natasha gained her own licence as a travel agent, and bought in her own computers. The company kept her busy and paid its way but did not make a large profit. In a bid to raise the profile of her company, Natasha booked space at our Moscow International Travel Show, one of the clutch of trade exhibitions that ITE Group was now organizing following the success of the Moscow Motor Shows in 1994 and 1995.

Then disaster struck. There was a political coup against the government leading to devaluation of the rouble, and no one travelled. Natasha had paid for tickets in advance but her customers were no longer there. She came to me explaining that she had to cancel her space because her company was hurt. Feeling sorry for Natasha, I gave her a refund and wished her good luck.

The rich man who had backed her business venture was still there to support her, but she knew that she would become bored if she gave up her company and had nothing to occupy her. Natasha and I went for a drink together but the spark of our past relationship did not rekindle. We both had our own partners and our own lives. More cynically, it also occurred to me that there was a recurring pattern in my relationships; when women were 'looking backwards' and stuck in a time-warp, I was usually successful with them and could give them a 'leg up'. Conversely, when they were striding ahead and were successful, they had little time for me.

Natasha decided to close down her company and, for the time being, to continue living with her rich protector. She was to tell me later that she had also wanted to have children at that time, but not with her present lover, saying that, deep inside, she had wanted me to be the father.

Her lover met with one of the six 'big men' or oligarchs, who were not only wealthy but also wielded great influence in the Yeltsin era over the government of Russia and its affairs. This particular oligarch was impressed, as many others had been before, by Natasha's beauty and efficiency. He knew that her business had failed but, since none of his had, he went on to ask her if she would be interested in running one of them for him. He had recently taken over a privatized airline that was supplied with fuel and food by a range of different companies worldwide. One of his first acts was to cancel the contracts of these service companies and to form his own worldwide service company, funded by US$30 million from Switzerland, to take over their services. He put Natasha in charge of the service company.

Natasha became established in the airline business. She worked hard to build up the service company and grew it into a US$200 million business. Natasha was at the peak of her career and was appointed a senior vice president.

Then business in Russia entered another period of political turbulence. President Boris Yeltsin fell sick, the Prime Minister resigned, uncertainty ruled and the oligarchs found themselves under attack from the communists. All businesses came under investigation. The communists accused the reformists of selling the country short and of privatizing state industries at prices that were too low. Many criticized but few put forward any rational solutions.

An inner group of oligarchs approached the Cabinet. They offered to pay for the re-election of Yeltsin and, together with the other oligarchs, lend the government US$5 billion. As collateral, they would accept the shares generated by the privatization of large state monopolies. The deal proposed was a complete rip-off. The government would never be able to pay them back in cash and would have to hand over shares at way below market value. This would mean that the oligarchs would be able to realise a vast profit either by selling them on or, after an interval, by independent public offerings on international stock exchanges. However, the government would now be funded and Yeltsin accepted the offer, not knowing that the government would never be able to repay the loan.

As a result of these transactions, national airlines were losing their monopoly. However, regional airlines expanded their fleets and started flying to all major Russian cities as well as international destinations. Natasha persuaded her company to bid for one of them in order to expand her service company by making it the supplier to them both. Business continued to boom.

Six months later came the Russian banking crisis, when US$100 billion was wiped off the value of the banks' assets. Russia was declared unable to honour its obligations by the World Bank and International Monetary Fund (IMF) and the bank accounts of Russian citizens were frozen. When the liquidators walked into the banks, everything – down to the last light bulb – was removed. Another Russian dream had crumbled to dust. Russians watched helplessly as their money was devalued, and the cost of living rose by some 400 per cent. Just as they were beginning to believe in the banking system, what had not been lost during devaluation was now snatched away through the banking crisis.

In 1998, the Prime Minister was replaced and the new Prime Minister felt that the situation could be corrected if the privatization of state monopolies was reversed and the cash taken back from the oligarchs. However, the financial institutions of the West cried 'foul'. The Russian stock market collapsed, exacerbating the financial collapse of the economies of South America and the Far East other than China.

President Yeltsin remained sick and Russia lacked leadership. Along came Primakov, his own man and a real patriot, as Prime Minister. He promised to investigate the oligarchs. All their businesses and assets were re-routed overseas and any realizable assets were siphoned off and deposited in Western banks. While the oligarchs lost part of their money, stability returned. Primakov was trusted by both sides and speculators started to return to Russia and the CIS. Attention began to turn to the 2000 presidential election.

In these uncertain times, Natasha decided to quit and cash in while she was still ahead. She made an amicable departure from her oligarch, having saved some US$10 million. She also owned houses in London, the US and the South of France and six apartments in Russia – one for her daughter and the others for rental – and continued to travel widely.

In November 1998, Natasha and I met again in London at the Millennium Conference Centre. Although we told each other that it was by chance, we both knew that we had contrived the opportunity to meet. In spite of all that had happened to each of us over the past seven years, we still had deep feelings for each other. Natasha believed that we could fall in love again but she was desperate to return to Russia. She felt the need to return to her roots to regain the feeling of security that even being a millionaire could not give her. She tried to convince me that my future lay in Russia too, with the opportunity to make even more money. However, I could not be convinced and told Natasha that I had taken the decision to sell my shares in ITE Group and live in London. Calling me a fool, she stormed out and took the next flight back to Moscow.

★

Now close to 40 and a veteran businesswoman, Natasha turned to politics and assisted in the re-election campaign of the Mayor of Moscow, tipped to be the possible future Russian President in 2000. He seemed to be neither pro- nor anti-West and appeared to look after everyone's interests. After her return to Moscow, Natasha took part in the redevelopment of the city and was given additional responsibility, as he wanted to extend campaign coverage over the entire country in order to enhance his prospects in the presidential election.

Once again, President Yeltsin dismissed his current prime minister and established another candidate whom he backed to fight in the mayoral campaign, in order to undermine the current mayor's power base.

However, after dropping out of the presidential contest the current Mayor was re-elected and Natasha began to think of leaving politics altogether. If Lushkov had won the presidency she might – who knows – have been appointed a Minister? Such is the stuff that Russian dreams are made of.

Today, Natasha is content living as the housewife to an artist-author with one child to look after and happily supporting her husband. She is part-time adviser to an international investment fund.

Chapter 7

Growing the Business

The second Moscow Motor Show was a smashing success, with over 200,000 members of the public attending. We were the talk of the town in the news, media and on TV. In counterpoint to our success, the country was battling with the World Bank for loans, while a free-for-all competition was erupting among the oligarchs to provide a solution for the development of Russia's wealth in energy, minerals, metals, agriculture and defence.

On a return journey to England, I shared a ride to the airport with an executive in the oil company BP. He expressed his frustration at being unable to make the right contacts in Moscow. I asked him why he didn't visit an oil show and network there. The executive told me that, as in communist times, the Moscow Oil Show was held only once every four years. When I suggested an oil conference so that people in the industry could meet each other more often, especially with so many changes in government and new ministers, the executive thought it was a great idea.

Through an Armenian friend of Edouard who worked for the Ministry of Fuel and Energy, I was able to solicit the support of the Ministry for the 1st Oil and Gas Conference because the ministers had visited the Motor Show and recognized the name of ITE as the organizer. After several months of waiting, we received the necessary permissions and quickly reserved the Congress Hall of the Moscow City Government Building. With just three months notice to sell and organize the conference, ITE launched a massive blitz of telexes, followed by fax campaigns inviting the 'who's who' of the oil and gas industry to attend and, in some cases speak, at this important conference. The response was excellent, aided by the fact that we had timed the conference to run at the same time as the NEFTEGAS (Oil & Gas) Expo at the new Expo-Centre, organized jointly by Nowea (the rival German exhibition company) and ExpoCentre.

In this manner, all those who attended our conference would also be able to visit the NEFTEGAS Expo without exhibiting. With over 600 paying delegates, we proceeded to buy 600 entry tickets to the NEFTEGAS event, which we included, free of our charge, in our delegates' packs. All went well until we were advised that our conference delegates would not be allowed to visit the NEFTEGAS Expo, in spite of the fact that they had tickets. This unwelcome development resulted from a unilateral decision by the Germans to intercept them at the Gate and deny them entry. The decision was quickly overturned by the management of Expo-Centre, which foresaw that it would be counterproductive to block the movers and shakers of the leading international companies in the oil and gas field from visiting their event. Besides, the attendance of the conference delegates would enhance their exhibition.

The Oil and Gas Conference, the first to be organized in Russia, was an undoubted success, but we were not through with unpleasant surprises. At the last minute, the advisor to the Oil and Gas Ministry demanded at least 40 per cent of the gross revenue from the conference instead of the 20 per cent to which we had agreed from the outset for their sponsorship. The balance of 60 per cent of the revenue left for ITE barely covered the basic overheads, such as hiring the venue, display materials and providing lunches and dinners, let alone providing a 20 per cent profit for ITE. The ministry official had no idea of the overhead costs nor, when I tried to explain their impact, were they particularly interested or concerned. Effectively, they had nationalized my conference. From this episode, I learned an important lesson: make sure that both sides understand clearly the nature of an agreement in advance. In this instance, the ministry's logic was simple: I had asked for their blessing and the ministry had given it, but with a price attached. I would have been better off to ask them for their sponsorship in return for a fixed fee instead of a percentage. Instead, I had paid heavily for my mistake.

While agreeing to pay the extra 20 per cent, I took the chance of asking the official whether for that additional charge I could be granted, in the form of a letter of endorsement, the blessing and sponsorship of the ministry for an international oil and gas show to follow our successful conference. In this way, I explained, he could help us to make up our losses on the conference. This arrangement, which he accepted, was his way of assisting us in our time of need.

The success of our first Oil and Gas Show was due in no small measure to our innovative marketing techniques. Previously, the oil and gas industry as a state-owned monopoly had been poorly organized and largely ignored. While ITE organized the show, we liaised with people in the industry to find out what they most wanted. By contrast, ExpoCentre and the Germans had weak marketing and did not bother to consult with anyone in the oil and gas business. As a result of participating in the organization of our show, people in the industry had played a part in its success.

We made it easy for Russian trade visitors to attend the show by providing transport from the airport and pre-paid tokens for the Moscow Metro. Both facilities, previously unheard of in Russia, proved to be excellent for public relations and encouraged thousands of engineers and officials to attend. We also provided food and drink tokens to all the Russian exhibitor stands as a gift – not an act of charity – to mark their participation in the show. These tokens, another first for any Russian show, were important to, and particularly appreciated by, the Russians because of the high prices for food and drink provided at the bars in the show, imposed by the owners of the new ExpoCentre, which were, frankly, exploitative.

I had recognized that under normal circumstances the Russians would be unable to afford either transport to the show or food and drink once there. The token system solved these problems at a stroke, enabling the Russians to participate fully and making the show the most successful that Russia had ever seen. The additional costs incurred by ITE were recovered from the international exhibitors who paid slightly increased fees, thereby effectively subsidizing the Russians. Many observers said that ITE would fail with the Oil and Gas Show because the international exhibitors were charged three times the amount they would have had to pay at ExpoCentre. In fact, the international exhibitors did not mind paying more because they were gaining exposure to a bigger audience than they would have at ExpoCentre. Conversely, the Russians were paying less than ExpoCentre charges. Despite the exhibitors' evident satisfaction, ExpoCentre and their German co-organizers continued to spread rumours that the international exhibitors were being exploited.

Once again, I realized that organizing exhibitions and trade shows in Russia was the perfect way to bring me close to those in power among the political élite. Now I started to look for ways to exploit this access in order to extend our business interests further. With the success of the first Oil and Gas Show under our belt, I approached ministers who attended the show with the suggestion that they might intercede with ExpoCentre in order to broker an agreement over the future staging of oil and gas shows in Moscow. Thanks to their intervention, an agreement was reached. In future, organization of the Oil and Gas Show would alternate between ITE, which would organize one year, and ExpoCentre, which would organize the next. The permanent location for the show each year would be ExpoCentre. This meant that we could return to ExpoCentre after our threat of 'banishment'.

An important and satisfactory feature of this agreement was that we were still able to continue holding our annual oil and gas conferences in Moscow and the CIS. Contacts at the expositions with oil ministers as conference speakers were quickly transferred into sponsorship events. As reported in the next chapter, we expanded beyond Russia with the launch of the 1st International Kazakhstan Oil Show and Conference, and the 1st International Uzbekistan Oil and Gas Show. With the assistance of other important ministers, we also organized the first Turkmenistan Oil and Gas Show, pursuing our oil and gas exhibitions development into India, China, Saudi Arabia, Bahrain and Jakarta. With the establishment of eight international oil and gas exhibitions, we were also able to organize conferences in the world's key business centres for the oil and gas industry.

Building on our success, we moved our London offices from the small house that we had occupied to four full floors of a new 12,000 square-foot building in Maida Vale, which were devoted to the Motor Shows and our own eight International Oil and Gas Exhibitions and Conferences. Our staff there – consisting of our office manager, Pamela, and a secretary – was supplemented by my step-daughter Stefania (Stefy), a trained architect and designer, who had previously performed the job of Production Manager for the *European Bookseller*. Initially, Stefy came on board to design brochures and then to publicize the shows. In those pre-Internet days, I hit upon the idea of sending faxes to publicize the shows rather than using more conventional mailshots or telephone selling – something that had not been tried before in the Trade Fair business. At that time, BT had recently introduced technology permitting the despatch of 10,000 faxes per hour over a single telephone line. We adopted this technique and elicited an excellent response, far better than any that telephone cold calling would have yielded. We also saved greatly on staff.

Stefy brought in a friend of hers, a young Australian backpacker called Mark Webber, and I engaged my elder son Mark to help him to organize the Moscow Oil and Gas Shows. Both proved to be very good at the job and stayed on, rather than leave the company. In turn, they brought in two of their friends to join the London office team. My son Mark also joined us in ITE after graduating from Syracuse University and played an increasingly important role in supporting me. Roddy and I ran the Motor Show, while the two Marks looked after the Oil and Gas Shows.

In Moscow, Edouard was in charge of the ITE office. His previous partner Nicolai took over as Director General of the Book Fair. However, Edouard and I could see the writing on the wall; the big money in trade exhibitions was to be made not from Book Fairs but from the Oil and Gas and Motor Shows. Edouard needed more staff in the Moscow office. As well as recruiting three new secretaries, he approached Mikhail, who had already helped me greatly in the early days of negotiation with the Association of Russian Publishers for their participation in the ill-fated *Salon International du Livre* in Paris. Mikhail, who had been the youngest-ever member of the Moscow Young Communists (Komsamol), was now Vice President of the Post-Soviet Publishers Association. He looked and sounded like a Westerner and, had the communist regime persisted, would surely have risen as a diplomat to the rank of ambassador. Initially, Mikhail was reluctant to join ITE, a capitalist organization, in the expectation that the old communist order would make a comeback. However, as everything descended into a state of chaos and it seemed that communism was doomed, he finally consented to join us.

I put Mikhail in charge of Russian participation in the Moscow Oil and Gas Show and assigned Edouard to the Motor Show. They moved out of the old, rather seedy book fair office into new offices in a fine old Tsarist building leased from the leading publishing house Khodostena Literatura that had published the Russian edition of John Le Carré's *The Russia House*.

Once installed in this beautiful building, ITE hired some of the people who had been made redundant as a result of the collapse of publishing in Russia. They were cultured people with foreign language skills, who were very correct in their business dealings; a welcome addition to the ITE Moscow team. ITE also took on Vladimir, the number two in Khodostena Literatura as Office Manager, while Mikhail was elevated to Director General. At the same time, Edouard, who did not like large organizations, made it plain that he wanted to be his own man and, as a reflection of his Russian character, have the time for music, women and good food while still delivering great results.

In 1994, between us we organized Motor Shows in St Petersburg, Moscow, Kiev, Kazakhstan, Tashkent and Prague, together with our own oil and gas event. Turnover had increased four-fold from the previous year and we traded under the name of Roddy's formerly dormant company ITE – International Trade and Exhibitions.

During this period, I ran into Dr Barbara Hanlon, a very nice Polish girl whom I had previously known and had parted from on a friendly basis. She brought me up to date with her activities as the London-based Sales Director of Convatech, the CEE division of Bristol Myers. As we talked, with my subconscious focused as always on trade fair business, I was struck immediately by a single thought: why not introduce medical shows? Barbara understood pharmaceuticals and the requirements of the medical profession; so surely here was the necessary expertise to help ITE organize medical shows in Russia and the CIS. Not long after her assistance in providing cholera vaccine for our first Oil and Gas Show in Kazakhstan, described in the next chapter, Barbara decided to leave Bristol Myers and join us at ITE.

Together, we organized the 1st Moscow International Healthcare Exhibition (MIHE), exploiting the time interval between the medical shows of ExpoCentre which were held every four years. MIHE was an immediate success, attracting over 76,000 visitors from all over the CIS. Not unexpectedly, when ExpoCentre saw ITE's success they decided to stage their own healthcare show every year in order to put MIHE out of business. Unfortunately for them, the Minister of Health was so impressed by MIHE that he agreed to sponsor the ITE show for five years. He also agreed to ExpoCentre putting on an annual healthcare show but stipulated sensibly that the two shows were to be scheduled four months apart.

Barbara maintained offices in both London and Moscow to sell the healthcare events and expanded her activities into Kazakhstan and Uzbekistan. She also helped me with the organization of the Bolnista (Hospital) Show in St Petersburg, where the main medical exhibition was organized by LenExpo. In the Soviet era, LenExpo had been controlled by ExpoCentre in Moscow but had been privatized following the collapse of communism and was now self-financed. I asked LenExpo's director if the Germans were investing in the exhibition centre. On being told that there was no German involvement, I offered to make an unsecured loan of US$2 million in return for ten year's exclusive rights to mount exhibitions at LenExpo on a wide range of themes including food, agriculture, packaging, construction and tourism. The loan would be repaid from future rental payments by ITE. I was delighted when my offer was accepted. Such a deal would have been impossible in Moscow.

With a secure foothold in St Petersburg, we came up with the innovative concept of test organizing our shows in St Petersburg and then transferring them to Moscow if they were successful, rather as a London theatre producer would try out a play in the provinces before moving it, if it was a hit, to the West End. Using St Petersburg in this way, as a prequel to Moscow, also served another purpose. While Moscow was the gateway to Russia, St Petersburg was also the gateway to the Baltic and CEE.

A construction show, staged first in St Petersburg and then transferred to Moscow, was highly successful. Barbara Hanlon and ITE took over the St Petersburg Hospital Show ('*Bolnista*'), run previously by the Germans. Within the next fifteen months, Barbara had graduated from organizing one medical show to staging eight major healthcare trade shows, with 900 pharmaceutical companies as clients, of which the biggest was the Bolnitza Hospital Show in St Petersburg. This achievement soon mushroomed into twelve annual exhibition and conference events, breaking all sales records and earning her a seat on the board of ITE.

The success of all these shows in Moscow and St Petersburg was an indicator of the rapidly expanding market in Russia. Some Russians themselves were becoming wealthier. During my summer holidays in Cannes, I noticed increasing numbers of Russian tourists in places where previously there had been none.

During its period of high growth in the mid-1990s, yet another major opportunity arose for ITE to expand its trade fair activities in Moscow. In 1995, while in Cannes, where I kept an apartment behind the Carlton Hotel adjacent to the 'Croisette', I noticed that the nearby city of Nice was staging a jet-ski competition in the form of a Nice–Cannes race. This sounded like a fun event, which would attract many of the 'movers and shakers' in cosmopolitan Riviera society and I decided to pay Nice a visit. On the evening before the race I met Gael Pineau, an impressively healthy French sportsman, who assured me that he was going to win the race. The next day he finished third but was in a good humour when I met him again after the race.

I had been thinking that although we organized trade shows based on all kind of themes, so far we had neglected boats and sports exhibitions generally. After lengthy chats and enthused by my promise of meeting beautiful Russian girls, Gael accepted my invitation to visit Moscow and have a good time. This is where I sprung the question, 'Gael, how would you like to run a Moscow Sports Show?' After a few nights out in Moscow, Gael had fallen in love with Russia and answered, 'IF we organized a travel and tourism show with it, that would make sense.' His suggestion was prompted by discussions with the Russian competitors in the Cannes jet-ski race with whom he had struck up a friendship. Having talked to them, he had come to realize that there were probably between 10,000 and 20,000 Russian holidaymakers in the South of France and many more in other locations, such as Cyprus and Turkey in Europe and the more well-known tourist destinations in Asia. Gael readily agreed to work on a travel and tourism show, taking a percentage of the profits instead of a salary. He knew absolutely nothing about exhibition management but rapidly showed himself to be a natural in the field.

I had recently approached the director of ExpoCentre to explore how our Moscow portfolio of shows might be extended. By now, management of the shows there was 'carved up' between ITE, the Germans and another exhibition company called Comtech, which was owned by a Russian entrepreneur. Comtech's shows covered computers, electronics, telecoms and fashion, while ITE covered oil and gas, motor cars, construction, security and health. In other words, ITE and Comtech managed all the big shows and we had agreed not to 'poach' each other's themes. Competition with the Germans remained fierce and they staged some seven shows at ExpoCentre, compared with ITE's five in Moscow. The ExpoCentre director now treated me with respect but I was still suspicious of his good intentions towards us. Accordingly, I asked him which additional theme he could give to ITE without 'hurting' the Germans. The director's response was that ITE could have 'Tourindustria', which he considered to be the worst unallocated theme, not imagining that my next move would be to stage a travel and tourism show. It seemed that the Germans were not interested in promoting tourism because they were not keen on encouraging holidaying Russians to settle in their country. The Germans' loss was my gain. ITE's Travel & Tourism Show, as Tourindustria became, would prove to be ExpoCentre's and Russia's biggest ever and most profitable exhibition.

Following Gael's commitment, I checked quickly with Expo-Centre for a time slot, only to discover that it was fully booked for the next year, except for seven days reserved for a gift show. I visited the current gift show and was amazed to find that the only gifts on display throughout a 5,000-square-foot hall were Matriochka – little Russian dolls.

I immediately accepted the challenge of taking over the organization of the gift show for the following year by re-titling it and providing two exhibitions side by side – The Moscow Tourism Show, with a gift section only, thereby providing space for our Sports and Travel Show.

Having first carried out some research homework, I also visited the Minister of Culture and Tourism to enlist his support. The statistics showed that 6 million Russians travelled abroad in 1994 and a breakdown of the numbers showed which countries were visited. Not surprisingly, Russian holidaymakers showed a preference for those countries, notably Cyprus, Greece and Turkey, that did not require visas to be issued in Russia but which issued them at their airports on entry. The minister was concerned at the extent to which Russians were spending money abroad and agreed that a Russian Tourism Show might help to staunch the outflow and encourage foreign holiday visitors to Russia.

Gael and I invited potential government exhibitors to participate in the 1st Moscow International Travel and Tourism Exhibition (MITT). We supplied them with travel statistics through their Ministries of Tourism and 115 governments replied. Following the demise of Intourist, the travel agency industry was blossoming; like Natasha, some 2,000 travel agents had set up businesses in Moscow and all were potential exhibitors.

The show layout included a series of government stands, each housing the travel agents from that particular country. The MITT turned out to be an effective interface between Russian and foreign tour operators. Over 116,000 members of the public and trade visited the show, delighted that they could view holiday destinations on video and book their holidays direct through one of the tour operators exhibiting. As with the Oil and Gas Show, ITE charged the international exhibitors a higher price, to subsidize the Russians in terms of transport and food costs, to facilitate their attendance and to make the show a resounding success.

The timing of Gael's concept was excellent and the MITT was an outstanding success, both financially for ITE, as its most profitable show to date, and for the exhibitors. A total of 80 countries participated and the show went on to grow in subsequent years to 30,000 square metres, earning the label of the world's most expensive show of its kind. The customers kept coming back year after year and the show was voted 'Best Travel and Tourism Exhibition of 1996'. Of course, ITE's triumph stoked the fires of the Germans' enmity. For example, Lufthansa, who did exhibit at the show, were deeply aggrieved at having to buy space from an English company.

Gael travelled to Canada to receive the award. His compensation was so much that he decided to cash in and sail his own boat to Corsica, a novel form of early retirement at the age of 38. For Gael it was not the money but the challenge that had driven him. He simply decided to go out and quit at the top the show which, even today, remains one of ITE's top revenue producers.

Business in Russia was booming. Virtually every exhibition theme we launched was successful. Roddy felt that it was time to set up a proper business organization in England to support sales and marketing. We looked at what others had done in the same field and studied the business model of Blenheim Plc – a public company that had grown dramatically in Europe by acquisition. However, what really distinguished their business from ours was their established 'brands' – the trade fair themes that they cherished year after year and were 'cash cows'. This continuing flow of business compared favourably with our one shot, hand-to-mouth approach, which had no guaranteed tomorrow. We had no secure tenure in Russia; in fact, we had barely finished one show when we started to negotiate the next year's tenure, often not securing a signed contract until two months before the show was held.

This type of risk-taking was unheard of in Europe, but then Moscow opportunities didn't exist in Western Europe either. Nevertheless, the time had come for us to put our house in order. We decided to approach Blenheim, which was chaired by Neville Buch – an experienced City man who had quickly grasped a thorough understanding of the trade fair business and whose company was listed on the London Stock Exchange.

Our first encounter with Blenheim was hardly auspicious and came about as a result of the relationship that I developed with a German travel agent called Christophe Renevier, whose business was based on making the travel arrangements for German exhibitors and visitors to Russian exhibitions. In retaliation for a German plan to launch a Motor Show in St Petersburg at Len Expo, which I considered to be an infringement of our turf, I pitched to take over 'Bautech' and 'Stroytech', both building shows run by the Germans. The problem for ITE was that 60 per cent of the exhibitors at construction shows were German. Therefore, a show organized by ITE in the construction field would attract few exhibitors and would most likely fail. One of my Russian advisers used a military analogy to explain to me what I needed to do in order to succeed. 'Use a pincer movement,' he said. 'Establish a German company, controlled by yourself from Moscow, to stage the show and attract German exhibitors.'

Acting on that advice and as a stratagem for infiltrating the German camp, I persuaded Christophe Renevier to become Managing Director of a new company – German International Trade

Fairs (GIMA) – registered in Germany and wholly-owned by German nationals. The company was formed by Christophe, who became both its Managing Director and part-owner. GIMA then announced that it would stage a construction show in Moscow.

GIMA ran immediately into problems following its bold announcement because the Germans already had an established construction show in Moscow. Christophe suggested that we should go to Blenheim as the owner of 'Batimat', the world's largest construction show, to stage a Moscow Batimat under licence and, therefore, give GIMA more credence. Blenheim turned us down point blank and decided to try to establish Batimat themselves in Moscow. When they approached ExpoCentre, they made a point of declaring that they had nothing to do with ITE. This turned out to have been an unwise move. The ExpoCentre director, with his habitually devious turn of mind, suspected that he was being tricked and that ITE was really behind the Blenheim approach and refused to lease any space to Blenheim. Without their protestation, Blenheim would have gained the booking it wanted.

Coincidentally, over several months during that period, Blenheim's new Managing Director, Steffan Svenby, was in the habit of visiting our offices to meet with Roddy. He wanted Blenheim to enter the Russian market but had problems with some of his board of directors who were wary of that market. Finally, and after much discussion, Roddy and Steffan came up with a great solution in the form of a licensing agreement for Batimat and a first refusal on other Blenheim titles for the CEE and Russia, in effect giving ITE carte blanche access to that part of the world. This generous act amounted to giving us the title deeds to a gold mine: being able to use the Blenheim name was like opening a Hilton Hotel where there had only been a state-run hotel previously. ITE would now be a serious contender.

We then managed to convince Neville Buch, the Blenheim Chairman, to license other major branded theme titles for Russia and the CIS for 50 years: Batimat, Maison et Objet, Securitec (Security) and Premier Collections (Fashion). As the consideration for introducing these well-known brands into Russia, we contracted to pay a small royalty based on revenues generated, equivalent to approximately 4–5 per cent of sales. In return, we received from Blenheim marketing know-how, data bank support and, most importantly, the right to solicit their enormous client list for the Russian market. As a consequence of these arrangements, Paul Hancock, the Blenheim Director of International Development, joined ITE.

All four expositions were introduced successfully in Moscow from 1995 and became blockbusters that were subsequently cloned in all the major cities of the CIS. Over the next two years, the four shows licensed from Blenheim grew to 12 shows annually. Having the Blenheim titles firmly within ITE's grasp, we announced International Security, Construction, Hotel Equipment and Food and Leisure shows to join our existing portfolio of Oil and Gas, Motor Cars, Medical and Tourism. Whatever was put on in Moscow was then 'cloned' in other locations such as Kazakhstan, Uzbebekistan, Kiev, St Petersburg and so on.

One of the conditions of the Blenheim licences was their strict quality control over the use of their name and brands in Russia. One incident that I will never forget occurred at the 1st Moscow International Securitec Show, when Blenheim's Managing Director, Peter Hazelzet, visited Moscow to see for himself how ITE was performing. Alas, and to all our surprise, the show opened with 250 international exhibitors all complaining that their stands were not installed or equipped. This was because the German stand constructor selected by Blenheim had been hit by a strike of the Russian stand fitters who had lost out in tendering for the business.

Chaos ensued in the exhibition hall, with 250 companies represented by 750 directors all sitting on their unpacked crates and other materials in their allocated spaces with neither tables nor chairs, unable to work. Peter, who had a special, made-to-order 'Blenheim' badge displayed prominently on his jacket, was attacked by disgruntled exhibitors, saying that they had relied on Blenheim's reputation when agreeing to exhibit, although the show had been organized by a Blenheim Licensee.

'Thank you, Roger. You are finished,' I was told politely but bluntly by Peter, who then packed his bags and retreated to France. The next three days of the exposition were a tragi-comedy: on the one hand, the exhibitors continued to complain vociferously; on the other hand, they were celebrating the excellent business that they were doing.

The 'proof of our pudding' was definitely in the 'eating'. When the renewal forms were distributed at the end of the show, 98 per cent made their reservations for the 2nd Moscow International Security Show on the assurance that ITE would use the Russian contractors in place of those previously selected by Blenheim. To ensure that we did not lose our licence, we asked each exhibitor to sign a form addressed to Blenheim indicating that they were pleased with the ITE organization, except for the stands, and stating that they had accomplished the results they had sought at the event. Peter was surprised at the renewal rate and these declarations of confidence, and our licence continued with his support. This incident was just one example of ITE's teething problems in our earlier years.

In the case of Batimat, its reputation and standing transferred easily from Paris to Moscow and it became the largest construction show (800,000 square feet) in Russia. As a German company, GIMA lured the German exhibitors into the Moscow Batimat and convinced the German government, which was unaware of

GIMA's British backing, that it should move on to take over the Paris Batimat Show. Within two years, GIMA's staff had expanded from two to sixty employees. Christophe started to represent German exhibitors who wanted to participate in ITE shows and GIMA became the second-largest company in Germany to organize shows outside Germany for German companies.

GIMA's success ultimately proved to be the last straw for NOWEA, the German exhibition company and our longstanding competitor in Moscow. Its market share plummeted from 76 per cent to just 20 per cent and NOWEA management accused ITE of being 'thugs in the payment of the Mafia'. In truth, one of the Germans' mistakes had been that they never took Russian partners; they simply relied upon using their money, when necessary, to buy influence. On the other hand, ITE engaged with Russian partners and did not, like the Germans, barge in and take over.

ITE's strategy was the only logical way forward; even with the support of ExpoCentre, the Germans were still failing.

NOWEA continued to fail in its efforts to displace ITE. One month before ITE's third Moscow Motor Show, which included a truck section, ExpoCentre announced, with German backing, that it would stage a truck show in order to take over some of ITE's success. I tried to convince ExpoCentre that competition of this kind would not work but the director was not open to reason. Accordingly, ITE announced a transport show, combining transport and freight that would take place six months before our Motor Show at the VDNK. Thanks to ExpoCentre's interference, ITE's Transport Show proved to be the biggest and most successful transport and freight exhibition in Eastern Europe. ExpoCentre's truck show was a miserable failure.

Next, the Germans tried to convince ExpoCentre to stage a specialized show about Interiors, which could have infringed upon the Batimat theme. Fortunately, ITE was protected by the trademark of Blenheim – a large and powerful international company – otherwise the Moscow Batimat Show could have been vulnerable. The German exhibition was no more than a mediocre success.

In London, ITE had moved again into larger offices – now on four floors – and had expanded its staff to 180. There were now about 25 staff in Moscow under Mikhail as Director General. Unfortunately, the success of ITE's operations in Moscow went to Mikhail's head. He declared that the Moscow office was now his turf and that we could get lost. With difficulty, I kept my temper and went back to London to discuss the Mikhail problem with our partners. They advised that it would be best to let the Russians sort out their own problems without interference from London. And that is exactly what happened. Mikhail had exceeded his own authority. The loyal Russian staff at ITE quietly had him removed.

Although Mikhail had acted out of character, I still had respect and regard for his talents and abilities. In order to turn the minus into a plus, I asked Mikhail to work abroad for ITE – a transfer that would protect him and his family. As his cover story, I sent him to Bahrain to organize the first Russian Trade Show to sell Russian products in the Middle East. If he was successful in the Middle East he could move on to London after one year. If unsuccessful, he could stay on in Bahrain. Mikhail was successfully tamed, and proved to be a great asset to us in London, where he was put in charge of all technical matters for all ITE's exhibitions worldwide.

Alex (of whom more on the next chapter) took over Mikhail's position through a newly formed Russian company that was now responsible for all Russian participation in all our shows, while ITE concentrated on the organization of all international participation. In that way we eliminated all inter-company misunderstandings before further problems arose. The new structure proved very effective and provided the Russian side with an opportunity

tre to contribute to Long Term Relations Between China and

British J.V. to Build
iness and Cultural City
London Docklands

new jobs for Great Britain. It is no less significant that these will include a majority of unskilled or semi-skilled jobs much needed in the Docklands area.

An-

The China Europe Trade been created ation with n plan- and

arts, a medical centre, a 4-star 200 room hotel, 120 apartment units, a Chinese street of individual shops, a cultural centre, residential units, a Chinese 'Harrods style' department store. The centre has made provision for parking for 1,000 cars. Many of the buildings will be decorated with traditional Chinese designs and built using

preliminary j/v agreement was signed between ICE Group and the China Council for the Promotion of Int'l Trade, and Tianjin Trust & Investment Corp., giving the go ahead to look for a site in either France, Britain or Germany.

In May of 1985 a 10 man delega' Inv

Municipal Govt of Tianjin fully supported the idea and

China's coming to
town with £25m

DOCKLANDS COULD BE THE GOAL

John Phelps

there were talks with the Chinese." carry out the venture by-passed

negotiations.

The new conference centre, which will have apartments and offices attached, is designed to spearhead a com-

the British

Leading them over
China's Great Wall

John Phelps

Y'S most success-issue of 1984? You see it in any offi-oles but Roger 's remarkable up has shown all ontenders a clean els as it has come where to a stock aluation of £55 n the past 12

year ago ICE was company which trade exhibitions in Nigeria, Kuwait, bia, the Lebanon China. Then Mr a London-based decided he really to better use his contacts in the public of China.

ITS LEAP

'Chinatown' planned for London river site

THE London Shipyard Development Organisation of the

Mr Shashoua has from Bekhor.

est has helped the e "a concrete cor-rm from what has been a conceptual

backs up his high-guage by disclosing

The entrepreneur says tha Western realisation tha China really means what says by an open door policy has turned a trickle of inter est into a collective stamped to get involved in th country.

"This process has at stroke significantly enhanced the value of our interests and we are now poised to take full advantage of our carefully timed entry to the market, he says.

HEAD START

"In this respect we plan to utilise what we believe to be a two-year head start to the maximum and the company is working on several exciting projects. Details will be released as soon as the visit ing Chinese delegations come to London within the next six months."

He believes 1985—the Year of the Ox will see

Above: Marie-Claude Shashoua, Lord Harold Wilson, Roger Shashoua and Premier Zhao Ziyang of People's Republic of China at the signing ceremony of the London Dockland China Centre.

Above: Roddy Shashoua (right) with Jiang Zemin, President of the People's Republic of China Centre at the re-opening of the China Aviation Show.

Above: Mr Shang, Chairman of Shenzhen Municipal Development Company, Roger Shashoua and Lord Wilson.

Above: (From left to right) Lord Wilson, Roger Shashoua, Jocelyn Barrow of BBC and Lady Falkender at the launch of the Shashoua Foundation.

1898-1989

Duckworth
G R O U P

CELEBRATING
90 YEARS
OF PUBLISHING
& HERALDING
NEW AREAS OF
EXPANSION

Colin Haycraft

Above: The Old Piano Factory, Camden Town, home of Duckworth's publishing operations since 1971.

Duckworth   SPRING HIGHLIGHTS

SEE US ON STAND
Nos. 119 & 136, LEVEL 2
AT THE LONDON INTERNATIONAL BOOK FAIR

GERALD DUCKWORTH & CO LTD
The Old Piano Factory, 43 Gloucester Crescent, London NW1 7DY
Tel: 01-485 3484, Fax: 01-485 2268, Telex: 896217

Above: The Czech Minister of Culture (right), at the official opening of the Prague Book Fair with Michael March – Director of the Prague Book Fair and Roger Shashoua.

1st
PRAGUE
International Book Fair and Writers' Festival

MAY 23-26,1991
PALACE OF CULTURE

SPONSORED AND CO-ORGANISED BY
THE CZECH MINISTRY OF CULTURE

For Reservations please call or fax:
Prague International Fair
2 Vale Court, 28 Maida Vale, London W9 1RT
Tel: (071) 289 4247 Fax: (071) 286 8620 Telex: 896217

Above: Mr Vaclav Havel, President of the Czech Republic visits the Faber Faber stand at the Prague Book Fair.

Above: Pavel Tigrid, Czech Minister of Culture at the Prague Book Fair.

Above: Prague Writers Festival and Book Awards.

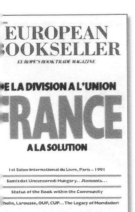

Above: Jeffrey Archer with Jonathan Reuvid
Publisher of European Bookseller.

Above: Roger Shashoua with Edwina Currie on the
Duckworth Group stand at the London Book Fair.

Ier SALON INTERNATIONAL
DU LIVRE ET DE LA
CULTURE EUROPEENNE

PARIS

14-17 February
1991

From left to right: Jilly Cooper, Alberto Vitale, Chief Executive of Random
House and Jonathan Reuvid, Publisher of the European Bookseller.

Above: Michael Palin at the
London Book Awards,
co-sponsored by the European
Bookseller.

Below: (from left) Moscow Mayor Yuri Luzhkov, Edouard, Manager of the Moscow Motor Show and a younger Vladimir Putin, future President of Russia.

Below: Mayor Luzhkov with Roger and Roddy Shashoua at the official opening of the Moscow International Motor Show.

Above: Moscow Motor Show attracts over 250,000 visitors.

Right: Mr Shoumeiko, 1st Vice President of the Russian Federation at the official opening of '93 Motor Show.

Above: The Ford stand at the Moscow Motor Show.

Above: (from left) Mr Rea, Minister of Transport, with Edouard and the adviser to the President and Roddy Shashoua at the official opening of the Kiev International Motor Show.

Above: Miss Ukraine opens the Kiev Motor Show.

Above: Ukraine military marching band at the official opening of Kiev Motor Show.

Above: Prague International Motor Show.

ve: (left to right) Prime Minster of Kazakhstan, Mr Nurlan
gimbaev, Mr Nazarbayev President of Kazakstan, with the
*c*tors of ITE at the Kazakstan Oil & Gas Show in Almaty.

Above: Mr Nurlan Balgimbaev, Prime
Minster of Kazakhstan (right) with Mr
Richard H Matzke, President Chervon
Overseas Petroleum Inc at the Kazakstan Oil
& Gas Show.

ve: The President of Turkmenistan, Mr
armurad Niyazov cutting the ribbon at
opening of the Turkmenistan Oil &
Show.

Left: Mr Danilov-Danilijan
Russian Minster of Ecology
& Environment giving his
welcome speech at Moscow
Oil and Gas Show.

Left: Mr Roger Shashoua
assisting Mr Shafranik,
Minister Fuel & Energy
Russian Federation at the
opening of the Moscow
Oil and Gas Show.

Above: (left) Mr Vyakhriev, Chairman
of GAZPROM with Roddy Shashoua.

Left: ITE's Sir Hugh Bidwell (left) accepts the Queen's Award for the ITE Group from Lord Bramall, the Lord's Lieutenant of Greater London, during a special ceremony in London.

Above: Roger Shashoua, Edouard and Mr. Sergey Stepashime Minister of Interior (now chairman Russia's Budget Committee) at the London Conferences.

Left: Victor Gerashenko, Chairman of the Central Bank of Russia (left) with Sir Hugh Bidwell, of ITE.

Above: Mayor of Moscow, Yuri Luzhkov participating in the ITE Moscow Invest '98 Conference in London.

Above: Mr Kostin, Director of International Affairs, Ministry of Interior of the Russian Federation (left), opening MIPS '98 with Edouard and show director Anna Wallis from ITE.

Right: The official opening of BatimatMosBuild '96 by the Minister of Construction, Mr Y Basin.

Below: Roddy Shashoua (left) with Boris Nemtsov, Deputy Prime Minster of Russia at Moscow International Travel and Tourism Show.

Above: Roger Shashoua at opening of the Moscow Travel and Tourism Show.

Above: Roger Shashoua celebrating another record year's growth.

Expomedia reports 80 per cent increase

Expomedia has announced almost double turnover in its six months ... 2005, reco...

opened during the year and another venue in Belgrade is due to open in December 2005.

The group also continues its ... strategy abroad,

Roger Shashoua, ... announced he will st... take up his new r... executive chairman fr...

He s...

Expocongress Amsterdam opens

NETHERLANDS - Expomedia Group launched its new EXPO XXI Amsterdam international expocongress centre on 26 May in the presence of the deputy mayor of Amsterdam and a champagne reception for 250 guests.

Ad Swartjes, chairman of Telegraaf Media Groep, Expomedia's Dutch partners, as well as Expomedia chairman, Roger Shashoua, attended the official opening

Ad Swartjes and Roger Shashoua

of events and the June programme includes the Dutch prime minister Jan-Peter Balkenende attending the economics ministry's FICCI IIFA Global Business Forum. The new venue will have hosted the Bollywood Oscars and an X-Box event within the first month of opening.

"The high level of interest and bookings for a wide range of events highlights the need for such a venue ... nue ...

overall response to the venue ... EXPO XXI Amster...

EXPO XXI opens in Cologne

Dutch media group Telegraaf Media Groep, meanwhile, has taken a 9.8m euro 10 per cent equity stake in Expomedia.

Expomedia and TMG jointly manage the newly opened 2,700m² events cent... XXI Amst...

Expomedia steps up global expansion initiatives

Russia - Expomedia Group has launched a new Licensing Division to identify new areas of potential growth in markets where it currently has no presence.

The exhibition and conference specialist firm will continue

aimed at increasing the size of Expomedia internationally.

The firm already has licensing agreements for China, Spain, France and certain regions of Russia, and in ...

and where the cost will be covered by the licensee.

Group CEO, Mark Shashoua says the firm believes it has proven its

date upon successful establish-ment.

He says: "We also see this concept as an important factor in the future development of the

... as companies

Telegraaf Media invests in Expomedia

Expomedia has confirmed that major Dutch media group Telegraaf Media Groep NV (TMG) has taken a 10 % equity stake in Expomedia.

TMG, which will appoint one non-executive director to the board, will subscribe for ... new ordi...

India next for Expomedia

How the Indian venue should look in June

...EDIA is opening its first venue in ... company will manage the Noida ...nal Expocentre, EXPO XXI in New ...hen it opens in June.

...state-of-the-art venue, with all the ...ities as our EXPO XXI venues

Indian market was that the quality of local venues was substandard.

Expomedia CEO, Mark ... India has one billion ... recognised exhibition cen... shows. "We are now al... international venue in ... growing economies in the ...

India Expo Centre gets going

India - The first shows have been held at the new India Expo Centre in Greater Noida, New Delhi. India International Interiors and India International Construction, organised by Expomedia and DMG World Media, took place at the end of April. The venue will officially open in the Autumn and follows a recent agreement between India Exposition ... ...h sees the latter les...

Shashoua shows the way

We drew attention to growth prospects of exhibitions and conferences group Expomedia in June, when the shares were changing hands for 137.5p and, since hitting 142.5p in Ju... the ...ight...ld ... has drifted ...

In our ...

Expomedia on the road again

Holland - The Dutch division of Expomedia Group, TE2, along with partners Telegraaf Magazines have acquired a 70 per cent stake in VDB Group, the Dutch publisher and event organiser for the car tuning and styling sector.

The VDB group currently organises 12 events in Holland, Germany and Bel... attract ...

In other Expomedia news, the first shows have been held at the new India Expo Centre in Greater Noida, New Delhi. India International Interiors and India International Construction, organised by Expomedia and DMG World Media, took place at

the end of April. The venue will officially open in the Autumn and follows a recent agreement between India Exposition Mart and Expomedia, which sees the latter lending its brand name to the site which will be known as India Expo Centre EXPO XXI.

Warsaw in driving seat at motor show

Poland - The fourth Warsaw International Motor Show 2004 saw a record number of visitors when it ran at the Expo XXI exhibition centre at the beginning of November.

Over 39,000 visitors, an eight per cent increase on 2003,

inaugural Miss Motor Show competition, we had live fashion shows everyday, the Pascar Car Audio competition with over 20 of Poland's leading car audio enthusiasts, and dance perform-ances by ...

Expomedia Partners with Gazprom-Media

Expomedia Group Plc has entered into a partne... ... ...

Good Food Show, are scheduled ... ...bor 2005.

Eyes on India for DMG and Expomedia

at the new EXPO XXI venue in New Delhi through a partnership agreement with IEM, the subsidi...

Former Reed Austria boss joins Expomedia Group

UK - Michael Stift has joined Expomedia Group as the commercial director of the Expocentres venue chain.

Stift is a former CEO of Reed Exhibitions Austria having joined the Reed Messe Wien in 1991 as managing director. This was followed by a stint as head of the Salzburg opera...

its venue expansion plans," says Stift. "I look forward to being part of the management team and to leading the chain of EXPO XXI venues to a point where their name is synonymous with the highest standards in facilities and service provision."

Expomedia CEO, ... says that Stift ...
...national ...

OLAND
XPO XXI Warsaw International
xpocentre

INDIA
India Expo Centre EXPO XXI in
Greater Noida

ERMANY
XPO XXI Cologne International
xpocentre

THE NETHERLANDS
EXPO XXI Amsterdam International
Expocentre

ERBIA
XPO XXI Belgrade International
pocentre

CROATIA
EXPO XXI Zagreb International Expocentre

Above: Prime Minister of India, Dr Manmohan Singh at the opening of the India Expocentre in Greater Noida.

Above: Mark Shashoua, CEO of Expomedia and Dr. Barbara Hanlon, Executive Director of India Expocentre at the official opening.

Above: (From right to left): Mr. Raj Manek Managing Director Expomedia Events India, Mr. Aggrawal President of ASSOCHAM, Mr. P.S. Rana Chairman of HUDCO and Ambassador K.V. Rajan.

Left: Roger Shashoua stepping down as Chairman to become Non Executive Director with Expomedia Group CEO Mark Shashoua.

Above: Michael Stift, appointed Group Managing Director of Expomedia Group.

Above: (from left) Roger Shashoua, Mr Soénius, Head of City Council for Finance and Economics in Cologne, Mark Shashoua and Christoph Renévier Managing Director of Expomedia Germany.

ɔ right: Azzelarab Hasnaoui, President of Expocentre Group with H.R.H King ɪmmed IV of Morocco and Roger Shashoua at the official launch of the Agadir Convention Centre.

Above: Roger Shashoua's dacha in Rubleskaya, Moscow.

Above: Roger Shashoua with his grandsons Armando and Samuel.

Above: Roger Shashoua with Tamara.

Right: Roger with Roddy Shashoua by his yacht in Puerto Banus, Marbella.

Chapter 8

From Russia and Beyond

Following the runaway success of ITE's second Motor Show in Moscow, it seemed timely to explore how we could build on that triumph with more motor shows or similar trade exhibitions in other parts of the former Soviet Union.

For our first expedition, Edouard took me to Kiev, capital of Ukraine, which was already striving for independence. The motivation for Edouard's journey was to visit his girlfriend, whom he had seen infrequently since his 'rise to fame' in Moscow. Unlike London with its two main airports of Heathrow and Gatwick, Moscow had almost as many airports as it had destinations. To take the flight to Kiev, we travelled to an obscure airport some one-and-a-half-hours' drive from the centre of Moscow. In this backwoods location, I was taken aback by the dilapidated state of the airplanes. Nevertheless, we duly took off and arrived unscathed an hour later in a Kiev that looked drab, grey and dull, even though it was spring.

Driving to our hotel in Kiev, I noticed automobiles stranded on the highway surrounded by many bottles of vodka. Were the drivers drunk, I asked? Apparently not. According to our driver, these people were trying to barter vodka for petrol. The conflict between Ukraine and Russia that had resulted from Ukraine's desire to secede had led Russia to 'turn off the tap' on petroleum supplies to Ukraine – a tactic that was used again more recently in 2006.

Edouard observed wryly that, with no petrol, Ukraine would be a lousy place to hold a motor show. On the other hand, I wanted to study Ukraine's potential. I was surprised to learn that this European country, with a population of 80 million, had no motor show, whereas Great Britain, with a population of no more than 55 million, had several, both large and small. On this comparison, I immediately suggested to Edouard that we should stage a motor show in Kiev.

I suspected that Edouard made up his mind about the possible location of any exhibition, according to the success of his social life. When he went to see his Kiev girlfriend, he found her resenting his long absences. To make things worse, while he had been busy acquiring 'movie star' status in Moscow, she had been two-timing him with a wealthy Georgian. After two days with his girlfriend, and realizing that things were not going to work out, Edouard came back to me and declared that Kiev was no place for a motor show. Anyway, he argued, it didn't even have an exhibition hall.

However, opinions were to change on the journey home. Kiev Airport was a nightmare, with Russian passengers going one way and foreigners, shepherded closely by Intourist guides, going another. Edouard and I were separated and did not see each other until we arrived at Moscow's Domedeva Airport. As I disembarked, I could see Edouard chatting up two women who, it turned out, were twins from Kiev that he had met on the plane. Now, he announced perversely, and somewhat drunkenly, that Kiev would be the ideal location for a motor show. I suspected that Edouard only wanted to go back to Kiev at the company's expense in order to visit one or both of his newfound friends. Therefore, I was pleasantly surprised when Edouard telephoned me two days after his return to Kiev to report that he had reserved space for the motor show at the Sports Palace in the heart of Kiev to be held at the same time as the Miss Ukraine Contest. It turned out later that Edouard had promised one of the twins that she would be voted Miss Ukraine. However, Edouard was infringing copyright by trying to usurp the Miss Ukraine contest; belatedly, his contest was re-titled 'Miss AutoSalon'.

Ukraine was in a condition of total chaos. When the staging of the Kiev Motor Show was announced, I found that there was no OICA member for Ukraine. Therefore, I went to the Automobile Association of Ukraine and asked them to appoint an OICA member that could sponsor the show. We also invited the Ukraine Minister of Transport to go to Paris, at our expense, to visit the Paris motor show so that he could see how things were done in the West. Although the minister did come to Paris, he declared on arrival that he would rather visit the Paris Air Show instead. Since the air show was some way outside Paris, Edouard and I decided to take him there on the Metro rather than spend money on expensive taxis. I explained that we were using the Metro so that the minister could gain an impression of the Parisian transport infrastructure, since he had admitted that this was his first experience of a subway train. It seemed to me that the minister's sole reasons for being in Paris were: first, to visit the West; second to meet up with his old cronies from Russia at the Air Show; and third to cream off expenses by staying in a 3-star hotel while being paid a 5-star allowance. I was probably right, but the minister was to show that he had hidden depths.

We began to think that the minister knew nothing about motorcars but my first impression of the man was not accurate. His interest in automobiles emerged during the long Metro journeys – 90 minutes each way – between Paris and the air show. When he could be distracted from the girls on the train, and told that he could not pick them up as he did at home by using his ministerial influence, he fell into long conversations with Edouard and me and we became good friends. At the air show, the minister succeeded in picking up two girls, which made Edouard and me quite jealous.

Finally, late at night in Montmartre, slightly drunk and singing Ukrainian songs, the minister gave his blessing to the 1st Kiev

Motor Show. He had responded to my simple reasoning and added his own rationale. 'The Ukraine only had Ukrainian motorcars. Production of Ukrainian motorcars had ceased. Cross-border car smuggling had started. Why not stage a Motor Show, legitimize the car business and give people a chance to buy a motorcar?'

By the time the Motor Show was staged, I was attracted to the secretary of the director of the Sports Palace at Kiev, and Edouard was reunited with his old girlfriend and had accumulated a 'stable' of 36 Ukrainian beauties who were finalists in the Miss AutoSalon Contest.

As with all Trade Fairs, the 1st Kiev Motor Show was peppered with bizarre and amusing incidents. When Edouard hired an airplane to drop leaflets over Kiev, it could hardly take off because it was so overloaded and it lacked windows that would open wide enough to throw the leaflets out except one by one. It would have been cheaper to distribute the leaflets by hand. As a promotion, Edouard handed out 'free' US$10 tickets; the Ukrainian recipients sold them rather than using them to get into the show. Notions of overnight security were primitive, to say the least. A man would be locked inside each vehicle overnight to make sure that no one stole it. Unfortunately, if he had been locked in from the outside, he was usually quite powerless to stop anyone from stealing the wheels.

At the opening, the political speeches, which should have lasted minutes only, droned on interminably for hours so that the exhibitors were tearing their hair out in frustration, while the public was locked out from the exhibition space. Inevitably, the 'heavies' also turned up. The show was the first in Kiev to have opened with military music. The biggest hit were the drum majorettes accompanying the military music, a particular favourite of Edouard, in spite of his complete lack of military service.

As I suspected, the sole purpose of Edouard's Miss AutoSalon contests was to allow him to meet girls. His system was foolproof. He would announce a contest – hundreds of girls would apply – and then he would interview each applicant with four simple questions:

- Are you married?
- Are you free to pursue a career abroad?
- If you had a great opportunity, would your parents stop you?
- Do you have a jealous boyfriend, who would not understand it if you had to work late?

The answers to these four questions pinpointed those who were vulnerable to Edouard's ploys and would effectively filter the applicants down to a shortlist. He would then take each chosen candidate out for the evening to check whether she behaved the same way at night as she had at the selection process during the day. As a result of this careful vetting, Edouard was able to fill up his address book with the telephone numbers and addresses of many beautiful girls.

For a fee, Edouard also provided girls to exhibitors as 'assistants', arguing that a pretty girl would attract people to their stands. Being on stands at exhibitions encouraged girls to believe that Edouard was pushing them forward in their careers. In reality, the only career being pushed forward was that of Edouard, who became very successful through his golden touch with the girls.

When the mother of one girl turned up at an exhibition, she found that her daughter had been locked into a cubicle on the stand 'to do some clerical work'. This had a practical purpose – it was a means of checking that the girl had brains as well as looking good. But there was also an ulterior motive in keeping them out of the way – so that Edouard could date girls without the others finding out. Using his scam, Edouard was constantly dating beautiful girls who thought that they were getting a leg up the career ladder rather than receiving a leg over from Edouard.

★

The Kiev Motor Show was very successful – attracting international automobile and autoparts manufacturers – and proved particularly popular. To the surprise of everyone, all the cars were sold off the stands and orders were taken beyond anyone's expectations. In Kiev, I also discovered that motor shows opened up another dimension. They gave me ready access to the local politicians because they were all hooked on motorcars, making it easy to meet all those in power at one event.

As so often in the past, my success was my undoing. The director of the Sport Palace realized that he would now be able to rent out space for Trade Fairs instead of just holding sports events. In the future, I would not be able to rent space there. To make matters worse, rather than congratulating us, the local automobile club announced a second motor show without any consultation. Edouard, being Russian, complained that after all the work the Russians had done, the Ukrainians were typically ungrateful. However, what we knew, and the Ukrainians did not, was how much work goes into the marketing and organization of such a show.

As a footnote to this saga, ITE returned to Kiev three years after pulling out when Kuchma became President. ITE was able to expand its themes then in a more favourable climate to foreign investors and became the largest trade fair organizer in Kiev.

After sorting out the various problems with our Moscow Oil and Gas Show, I sent Mikhail, then Director General of ITE in Moscow, and my son Mark to Kazakhstan, to secure the necessary endorsement from the Kazakh Minister of Oil to hold an Oil Gas Show in Almaty, Kazakhstan's capital. On arrival, Mark and Mikhail met with the minister, who had received a letter from the Minister of Fuel and Energy in Moscow, providing a reference for ITE and stating that he had been favourably impressed when he had visited the Moscow Oil and Gas Show. The Kazakh minister then dealt a severe blow to his two visitors. Just one week earlier he had signed a five-year contract with the Germans to stage Oil and Gas Shows in Almaty. He felt that it would be advantageous to use the Germans because it reinforced Kazakhstan's independence from Russia; the Germans would organize the show in Almaty, while ITE would organize it in Moscow.

Mark and Mikhail flew back to London. Mark was totally disheartened and felt that he had failed. However, he brought back with him a map of Kazakhstan, which I had always assumed to be a tiny, obscure place. One glance at the map showed me that, in fact, it was bigger than the whole of Western Europe. I realized instantly that just because the Germans had got in first, that did not mean that ITE was out of the frame. On the other hand, I was worried that if the Germans gained a foothold in Kazakhstan, they might seek to take over the Moscow Oil and Gas Show completely.

The ITE-run show had been truly international and that was its unique selling point, whereas the ExpoCentre show was Russian only. My fear was that if the Germans merged their Moscow and Kazakhstan shows, they might squeeze ITE out of this very lucrative market. I had to act quickly.

By chance, I had met Russia's first millionaire in London, Artiom, who had escaped from Moscow two months previously after being branded by Gorbachev as an 'opportunist'. When I met him, he was in the process of suing *Forbes* and *Fortune* magazines for libel because they had accused him of stealing money from Russia, rather than making it through his own efforts. Artiom won the case and, when Yeltsin took over the presidency, was able to clear his name in Russia. I explained our situation in Kazakhstan and asked him for his help. 'How,' I queried, 'can we bid for the contract if the Minister of Oil is certain to say "No"?' I was in luck. Artiom was well known there and was organizing a trade mission to Kazakhstan, including British Aerospace and other prominent companies, for which he was lead consultant.

Artiom told me that he was too busy to help directly but that he had a consultant called Alex, a Russian working for him in

Kazakhstan, who had many contacts there and who, by chance, happened to be in London that very day. In return for his help, Artiom asked for a percentage of any business that ITE might gain as a result of Alex's intercession.

Alex, whom I met later that day, reflected that it was a pity that I had not come to him in the first place when I was thinking of operating in Kazakhstan. He asked Mark and me to pack our bags so that we could fly out immediately with him to Kazakhstan. The flight to Almaty via Moscow took eighteen hours and was gruelling. Recovering in my hotel room, I realized that there was a strong likelihood that the Germans had never actually visited Almaty in person when negotiating the contract. The deal might well have been done on a government to government basis, working through the auspices of their respective embassies. Whereas the Germans were able to work through a government agency and were therefore well resourced, ITE was a private company with more limited resources. Pondering on this scenario, I thought it could be turned to our advantage.

The Kazakh Minister of Transport whom Alex approached was one of his good and trusted friends. At his office, Alex asked for help to gain access to the Minister of Oil so that he could put the case for ITE. He wanted to convince the Minister that ITE was a much better bet for Kazakhstan than the Germans, because its events were truly international, whereas the Germans were only interested in pushing German products.

There followed three days of meetings between Alex and the Minister of Oil, from which I was told to stay away until the final session. Thanks to Alex's skilful negotiations, a contract with ITE to organize the 1st Kazakhstan Oil and Gas Show was agreed and signed.

The German's contract was torn up, ostensibly because they had not followed through with their obligations. ITE now had a chance to prove itself in Kazakhstan, but we realized that we were not yet home and dry.

The Kazakhs had demonstrated that they could change their minds on a whim.

Oil was, and still is, Kazakhstan's only major resource and at that time was still firmly underground. The world's major oil companies, with Chevron in the forefront, viewed Kazakhstan as the new Saudi Arabia and were clamouring to invest billions to establish themselves there. The circumstances were ideal for ITE to run the Oil and Gas Show. Even if the contract lasted for only one year, it was sure to prove lucrative.

I turned over the running of the show to Mark. Over the next few months, he was to learn more about the business than most people would in a lifetime. Back in London, Mark recruited a staff of four and the team set off for Almaty to organize the Oil and Gas Show, which was also its very first Trade Fair. The first task was to book space at the Atakent Centre, which was basically a building for the local bazaar and which we planned to transform into a location suitable for a 10-day oil and gas event.

Kazakhstan was to prove an ideal training ground for Mark because of all the unforeseen disasters that occurred. Just 30 days before the show was due to open, Mark found himself in an impossible situation. The borders between Kazakhstan and its neighbours were closed because of a cholera epidemic. Arrangements had to be made to vaccinate all the drivers. Trucks carrying the materials needed for stand construction from Moscow to Almaty were attacked by Chechen rebels and other mafia groups as they passed through the mountains. Equipment had to be flown in because the trucks could not get through, so that costs quadrupled.

Mark needed 2,000 rooms for the exhibitors and visitors to the show and yet only a handful were available in a city that had never experienced such an influx of visitors before. The restaurants offered Mark extensive menus and then admitted that they could not provide all the dishes because they did not have any supplies of ingredients. To make matters worse for him, Mark lost ten kilogrammes in weight. When asked how he had lost so much weight in just a few weeks, Mark's reply was 'Something moved in the soup.' Ironically, because the international media had hyped Kazakhstan as the site of the new gold rush and although the borders were closed, the Oil and Gas Show was completely sold out.

ITE's Almaty operations, run by Mark with the help of Alex, were headquartered in President Nazarbayev's sanatorium, where they carried on their planning surrounded by sick people. It became apparent that the show was more than sold-out; it was over-sold. Mark had to order two more complete display centres from the Netherlands, to be shipped via Moscow. The truck driver bringing the Dutch display centres, having braved the mountain passes and penetrated the closed border, arrived in Almaty only to discover that he could not locate ITE. Instead of making enquiries, he simply turned around and drove back to Moscow. ITE had to hire a massive Tupolev freight plane to fly in the display centres to Almaty. They arrived just in time.

Other truckers hired to carry materials to Almaty said they wouldn't go because of the cholera epidemic and because the border was closed. I solved the first problem by contacting Dr Barbara Hanlon, who arranged to buy cholera vaccine through her contacts at Bristol Myers. The plan was to ship 2,500 shots to Russia and Kazakhstan and supply them to the truckers and any other workers involved in the Oil and Gas Show. Then the truckers, in turn, would be vaccinated and could keep the empty vaccines bottle to show to the border guards as proof that they had been vaccinated. The whole problem with the truckers was exacerbated by ExpoCentre in Moscow, which owned half of a company called Expoconsta – the latter constructed exhibition stands. I thought that by using Expoconsta it might endear ITE to ExpoCentre. How wrong I was. Expoconsta deliberately spread rumours about the cholera epidemic to 'wind up' the truckers. Only by visiting the director of

Expoconsta was I able to stop his company from undermining our transport link with Almaty.

As it turned out, the cholera epidemic was more of a political than a medical phenomenon. Kazakhstan was using it as an excuse to close the border with Russia and ITE was caught in the middle. Fortunately, Alex's link with the Minister of Transport proved invaluable once again and the closed border was opened to let ITE trucks drive through. As for the vaccine shipped out of London, we discovered that most of the truckers sold their shots rather than using them.

The Germans also got into the spoiling act. They spread rumours in Moscow to the effect that ITE's trucks were carrying guns and other equipment to be used in destabilizing Kazakhstan. The insurgency going on in neighbouring republics gave some credence to the rumours. All the materials that ITE was sending to Almaty – stands and exhibition goods – were consolidated and packed in Moscow. As these rumours spread, everything had to be unloaded and checked to show that there were no firearms or other illicit materials included. Of course, this process delayed shipments even more and made Mark's deadline even tighter.

All the major oil companies – Amoco, Chevron, BP, Shell, Total and so on – were contacted to see if they wanted ITE to arrange hotel rooms for them. They were all working with the Kazakh Government in developing its oil business. Unfortunately, they thought that the Kazakhs were making reservations for them while the government thought that the oil companies were booking their own rooms. Consequently, just a few days before the show was due to open, rooms were still needed for 600 key people, including CEOs. ITE was blandly 'economical with the truth' in order to make sure that everyone turned up and that the show would be a success. In fact, there were only enough rooms for the CEOs; any other key personnel would have to be content sleeping on the floor any old place.

★

When the time came, there were only 800 actual hotel rooms. Two oil companies competed to share rooms. Others slept in the sanatorium, which took on the appearance of a refugee camp.

Staying at the sanatorium imposed other inconveniences, such as the uncertainties involved in using the telephone. There was no fixed per minute charge for long-distance calls, which all had to be made through an operator from a booth in the sanatorium lobby. Telephones in the rooms could be used only for local calls. The operators were big, broad women, and the trick was to be nice to them so that they would give you a favourable rate. If you were really nice, instead of paying US$10 a minute, you might be charged only 10 cents. There was also no timing device, so that the operator would either guess or ask you how long the call had lasted; and that was negotiable as well.

To ensure the best result, I learnt to greet the operator each morning, asking after her health and telling her what a marvellous place Kazakhstan was. Instead of saying that I was making a business call, I would tell her that I wanted to call my wife to tell her how much I missed her and how much I wished that she could visit this beautiful country. I would then book my call for one minute and – because it was apparently a family matter – the operator would let me have fifteen minutes. This was the way to have a cheap business call. Conversely, if, say, an American delegate came in and demanded impolitely to make a business call, she would charge him over the odds. As so often in strange lands, a little applied psychology goes a long way.

There were further hazards and irritations in attending an exhibition in Almaty at that time. Only 50 per cent of the exhibition equipment was actually in place; executives were observed stealing equipment from each other's stands and fighting over chairs. More generally, there was a dearth of any electrical equipment – from computers to light bulbs – a seeming paradox when

Kazakhstan boasted a launch pad for rockets. Delegates had to bring with them everything they needed. Only the local medicine seemed to be more effective than the Western equivalent, as Mark discovered to his benefit after the soup episode.

Perhaps the greatest drawback to the bazaar as an exhibition venue – certainly, in terms of delegates' comfort – was that there were no toilets.

The first counter-measure was to tell delegates to be sure to relieve themselves before leaving their hotels. The only alternative was not to urinate or defecate inside the bazaar, but outside behind the bushes. One enterprising local Kazakh woman recognized a gap in the market and started to sell toilet paper by the yard to delegates. The price to those who were obviously American or European was US$1 a yard; for Kazakhs or Russians, it was just 5 cents.

There were frustrations also in attempting to advance business discussions outside the exhibition. If you made an appointment with a Kazakh and were late – even by five minutes – you were automatically in the wrong and the meeting would be cancelled. If a Kazakh was late, it was of no consequence and was treated as simply part of the culture.

Powerful Kazakhs were accustomed to call urgent meetings at short notice. Strangely, they always seemed to be in restaurants with their girlfriend in attendance. At the 'urgent' meeting, the Kazakh would consume copiously, ignore any business topic and flirt with the girl. Having taken his fill, he would then depart, thanking his Western guest effusively and leaving him to pay the bill. His mission was accomplished.

Nevertheless, the show was a major financial success, and in spite of all the problems and lack of accommodation, all the exhibitors booked to come back the next year. Among the multitude of lessons that Mark learned in such a short time was the truth that clients will forgive everything if they do well.

★

In the wake of the motor show successes in Moscow, St Petersburg and Kazakhstan, Edouard persuaded Roddy to organize
some more of the same in Romania and the Czech Republic.
Alongside the heavy German investment in the Czech Republic's
automobile industry, including the acquisition of Skoda by
Volkswagen, the Germans had already established a successful
motor show in Prague. However, they had alienated their local
Czech staff by regularly insulting them and belittling their efforts.
As a result of these poor human relations, the Czech staff revolted
and set fire to the German's exhibition. By default, ITE was able
to ride to the rescue and take over the show on a five-year contract, making it an even greater success.

Sadly, ITE's success was short-lived. When the Prague Motor
Show had finished, the Germans convinced the Czech Minister of
Culture that they had much greater financial 'clout' than ITE and
that they should be allowed to return and to run future shows. The
minister agreed with them and, despite its five-year contract, ITE's
organization of the Czech Motor Show came to an abrupt end.

While all this was going on, Jiri, who managed ITE's technical
team in Prague, was approached by the Czech Government to
take up the appointment of Director General of the Palace of
Culture. Initially, I was pleased about this development because I
felt that Jiri would be a useful contact and would help to safe-
guard ITE's best interests. However, my pleasure was replaced by
dismay when, as his first act in office, Jiri cancelled my long-
established Book Fair for alleged non-payment of fees, as well as
supporting the minister's cancellation of ITE's contract to run the
Motor Show. At a press conference in Prague, I showed the audience of media reporters confirmation that the cheques for the
Book Fair had been cashed, as well as a copy of the management
contract. When the press contacted officials at the Palace of
Culture to check out what I had asserted, they acknowledged that
the Book Fair fees had been paid. So why had Jiri bitten the hand
that fed him and done the dirty on me?

Once again, the whole thing turned out to be political. Our old enemy, the former Minister of Culture and now Speaker of the Czech Parliament, was playing a background role. His wife, a writer manqué, wanted to own the Book Fair herself, and had offered a deal to Jiri to be her partner in the enterprise, in order to get what she wanted. There was nobody in our corner to uphold ITE's rights.

We decided to go ahead with our Book Fair but at another, smaller venue. The former Minister instructed Czech publishers not to exhibit at the ITE Fair but to maintain the integrity of Czech culture by showing their wares at his wife's Book Fair. When questioned, Uhde denied that his recommendation had anything to do with his wife's involvement. He claimed to be simply supporting the Czech-organized show. Czech writers and publishers were disappointed by the turn of events because they wanted to network at a truly international show and not just a national event, which is what the Palace of Culture Book Fair would become.

In an unexpected twist, the organizers of the Frankfurt Book Fair decided that the former Minister had gone too far. They announced that in order to be impartial they would participate in both Book Fairs in the current year, but that they would not participate in the ITE event the following year. This sounded the death knell for the ITE Prague International Book Fair, which had been my first success in the CEE. Without any German participation, the fair could not succeed and I knew that the former Minister, having been challenged once, would put up even greater opposition to ITE in the future. Even Vaclav Havel, having championed the 1st Prague Book Fair and Writers' Festival, offered no support. Important political implications could be read into this small incident. I concluded that Havel no longer had power and was now a figurehead president, while the hard-liners who had been ousted by the Velvet Revolution were steadily re-entering politics. I feared the independence that writers and publishers had gained under Havel's leadership was now being steadily eroded.

★

In the meantime, the 1st Bucharest Motor Show had taken place and proved to be a great success. ITE applied to stage the second Motor Show the following year. Following an all too familiar pattern, the exhibition centre RomExpo had other ideas. They announced that they were taking over and would stage the show the following year themselves. In the end, neither show took place. Instead, the local dealers got together and organized their own event on a smaller scale in a disused aircraft hanger.

From Romania I moved on to Bulgaria to organize the Sofia International Book Fair and Writers' Festival as a clone of those that we had staged successfully in Prague and Bucharest. There, at the Academy Publishing house, I met Slava, an old acquaintance from the doomed Paris Salon International du Livre, when Bulgaria had been among my strongest supporters. Slava offered to introduce me to the Minister of Culture and was very useful in introducing me to other influential people as well. At the time, she was going through a divorce and her mind was on other things but she still found the time to give me her full support. I was intrigued by the honesty of the Bulgarians, who told me openly that they would take over the show if the first event was a success.

Unfortunately, much to Slava's disgust, they started to squabble about who would own the Book Fair when they took it over and how they would divide the spoils. In the end, there was so much in-fighting that I decided the Book Fair could not possibly go ahead. The same fate befell my attempt to organize the Sofia International Motor Show. I concluded that Bulgaria was just not ready for a free market and foreign inward investment.

The best feature of my foray into Bulgaria was that Slava and I became close friends and she continued to be most helpful. Slava proved to be a great asset for ITE – she spoke fluent Russian, understood the Russian mentality and played an important part in building up my interests in Russia and other parts of the CIS.

Back in Moscow, after my various adventures in Ukraine, Kazakhstan, the Czech Republic, Romania and Bulgaria, I reflected on the outcomes. It seemed that wherever and whenever our exhibitions did well there was always the constant threat of them being taken away from us, even when contracts had been signed.

Although, in principle, communism had fallen and command economies were supposed to be giving way to market reforms, those in power still had a monopolistic mindset. Capitalism, without the rule of commercial law, was still in its infancy.

Chapter 9

In Praise of Women

Some people who work and travel abroad extensively catalogue their recollections in terms of the scenery, architecture, national culture or the performing arts; others take hotel accommodation or local wines and cuisine as their benchmarks. In my case, my recollections of Russia and the CIS countries in the 1990s are encapsulated in my encounters related in this chapter with the many interesting and beautiful women that I met from Moscow to St Petersburg and from Kiev to Antalya. In all cases, they made direct contributions to the development of my business. Above all, these experiences and relationships were an important part of the learning curve in my search for knowledge and understanding of national characteristics and approaches to business, wherever my travels took me. But first, some general observations about women in Russia and elsewhere and my relationships with them during the 1990s.

When I first arrived in Russia, with a typically Western mentality, I was searching for a 'trophy girl', a companion on my business trips and 'arm candy' to impress my Western colleagues. I knew that I could never be like Hugh Hefner of 'Playboy' fame and secure such beautiful girls in the West. However, I knew how to charm, to say the right things and how to get my way. In Russia, with a gloss of sophistication unfamiliar in Moscow at that time, I felt sure of myself and I succeeded.

Friends and acquaintances often question my preoccupation with women as the accompaniment to my business adventures and the reasons why I always went out with many different women. I can assure them that I do not suffer from 'Portnoy's complaint', but there is certainly a craving for security, acceptability and companionship from women embedded in my psyche. I feel that my need probably stems from my early life when, at the age of fifteen, I was cast adrift from home and my mother's care and support, and was despatched alone from Egypt to the United States with the mission to restore my family's fortune.

Undoubtedly, women have helped me forget my problems far from home and at work and have provided relaxation and comfort at the end of long days of hard negotiation and deal-making in unfamiliar and often hostile environments. They have always played a supportive role, believing in me and my ideas.

Over time, I have realized that my relationships with women in foreign lands became more valuable to me professionally than the men with whom I was dealing. In Russia, particularly, I found women to be more reliable and trustworthy. Women were like my 'guardians'. They 'kept an eye out' for me, knew the major players in authority and in the shadowy business world I sought to enter and understood how and where they worked. They fed me with information and support, while I learned from them and, through them, came to understand and appreciate the Russian mentality.

In return, I was able to help my female companions: either financially, emotionally or professionally, as in the case of my friend Natasha, whose personal odyssey is featured in Chapter 6. From a mercenary point of view, there was always a good trade-off for both parties. From Natasha, too, I learned that Russian women friends are always there for you, even when they have a string of admirers.

The New Russian woman knows how to be 'feminine'; she uses her charm to attract the men who will help her further in life. She is good fun; she smiles and laughs a lot and provides a man with a sense of wellbeing, of security and confidence. The therapy certainly worked for me.

In summary, the younger generation of New Russian women today are products of a free economy. Some, under 25, may still take the advice of their mothers and learn from the older generation's experiences. However, they are more independent, less reliant on men and more career-orientated, often – like Natasha – running their own companies.

Today, girls from the big cities, like Moscow and St Petersburg, are more sophisticated and tough, but you will still find attractive women from the provinces, such as Nizny Novgorod, Samara or Volgagrad, who are eager to please and be helpful.

During the period from 1994 to 1997, I spent much of my time in Moscow, which was the base of our business operations. I made several trips to Moscow after the cancellation of the Book Fair, and Edouard took me to the reception of another exhibition organizer at the VDNK who was staging a textiles fair. Among the guests, Edouard noticed a girl from Georgia that he had known for some time who was there with a girl friend.

Confusingly, they were both called Galena. The friend looked pleasant enough but her manner was very cold. The four of us chatted together and Edouard suggested that we all went out for dinner after the reception. There was the usual indecisive discussion about where to go and, in the end, we dined at the hotel where I was staying. This time I was booked into the Flotel, a small cruise ship now converted into a hotel and moored next to ExpoCentre.

Flotel was a clever solution to the severe shortage of accommodation in Moscow at that time and was a good example of the early activities of entrepreneurs who were moving into Russia as the constraints of the old order disappeared. Flotel was owned by Tassos, a member of a Greek shipping family who had left Greece to make his fortune in Russia. Only one month after the fall of communism, during which time gambling had been banned, Flotel already had a rather basic casino. The atmosphere on board Flotel, which had about 80 rooms, was friendly and frequented by Moscow's *nouveaux riches*.

Edouard parked his Lada next to the gangplank and the Flotel bouncers let me on board, since I was a guest, but stopped Edouard and the two Galenas from entering. After a lengthy discussion, standing around in the snow on a bitterly cold evening, a payment of US$50 secured their entry. The management ruled that they could have dinner with me but that the three non-residents would then have to leave.

The cost of dinner was exorbitant – at about US$50 per head – and yet the dining room was full. By 10.30 pm, we had finished our meal and decided to go on to the disco. Tassos helped to manoeuvre us past the bouncers. In the disco we had a drink but Galena No 2 was still behaving coldly and speaking little. I found out that she had recently separated from a high-ranking political figure in Georgia. And then the music from '*Fame*' was played. Suddenly, this aloof figure kicked off her shoes, took to the dance floor and started dancing in a totally uninhibited way with Edouard's girlfriend. Afterwards, whenever I offered her a drink, she refused, which was something very unusual for any Russian, let alone a Georgian.

At the end of the evening, Edouard took off with his girlfriend. I asked Galena if I could see her home. I was concerned how I would get back to the hotel and asked her if I could spend the night in her apartment – in a totally platonic way – a quite normal occurrence in Russia. The building in which it was located was ugly and forbidding, but the apartment itself was very neat but tiny. While Galena made me tea, I noticed that the furniture consisted only of one big bed, a chair and a chest of drawers. In addition to the main room, there was a small kitchen and a bathroom. I started to drink my tea and Galena went into the bathroom.

Quickly, I undressed down to my T-shirt and baggy shorts, discarding the several layers of clothing that I was wearing to keep out the Moscow cold, slipped under the duvet and pretended to be asleep. When Galena returned from the bathroom, she asked me if I had drunk my tea and then, surprisingly for one who had been so withdrawn, burst out laughing. The sight of me in my shorts was too much for her. 'This is unique,' she said and called me 'Mischka' ('little bear').

Galena started to talk about herself. She was 28 and had met her husband when she was a student in Georgia. They had divorced after two years and she had become the girlfriend of a top politician from whom she had recently separated. Her mother lived in Georgia; her father was dead. After leaving her lover, and as an only child, Galena had decided to come to Moscow to visit her friend and to make a new life for herself. Her ex was a powerful man, and she had to get away from Georgia. Although I had little experience of Russian women then, Galena appeared to me to be 'upper class', having poise and wearing good-quality clothes. When she undressed, I noticed that she was wearing a La Perla bra and knickers, which was unusual for a woman living in Moscow.

At about 2.00 am, I moved to one side of the bed, curled up and went to sleep. There was clearly no warmth of feeling between us. But at 4.00 am she thumped me on the back, told me she couldn't sleep and asked me to hold her. I found that she had taken her underwear off and she was very beautiful. We made love but it was a very cold and clinical exercise on her part. I felt that Galena was using me so that she would be able to sleep. She disengaged, turned over and fell promptly asleep.

In the morning, I telephoned Edouard from her apartment and told him that I would take a cab to the hotel for that day's meetings. I got lost wandering around the grim Stalinist-era concrete apartment blocks but finally found a taxi. The fare charge was US$30 for a trip that should have cost US$1. In fact, Galena's apartment was so close to the hotel that I could quite easily have walked.

At midday Galena called me. 'Would you like to see the sights?' she asked. We met for lunch at 3.00 pm. Dressed in a tweed jacket, polo neck sweater, jeans and boots, she was indistinguishable from a smart, well-heeled Westerner. Galena said that she was busy that evening; so I asked if I could see her later. She said that she would call. Like an idiot, I waited in vain by the telephone in my Flotel room all evening.

Next morning, Sunday, I telephoned her to arrange to meet around lunchtime, as I had to catch a flight back to London in the late afternoon. At midday, Galena arrived; but it was the wrong Galena. For some reason – perhaps a sign of my agitation – I had telephoned Edouard's girlfriend by mistake and had not recognized her voice. At first I thought that she was there by pure chance and asked her where Edouard was. Then I realized my mistake. Anyway, we had lunch and I then took her to the dollar supermarket where I bought two bags of cakes and other goodies; one for her and one for 'my' Galena. I also gave her my London office number for the other Galena to call me when she had received her package. Otherwise, I would hope to see her the next time I came to Moscow.

Back in London, three days passed but Galena did not call. On the fourth day she did telephone me but was put through to a secretary in the ITE office who thought that she was just another client. It was only when I asked my office staff if anyone called Galena had telephoned from Russia that the secretary remembered. I called Edouard immediately, asking him to get in touch with Galena to tell her that I would be back in Moscow in a few days and wanted to see her.

One week later when I arrived at Moscow Airport, I was amazed to find Galena there to meet me. She had a car and invited me to visit her friend's dacha. We had the place to ourselves, took walks in the pine forest and drank tea on a bearskin in front of a roaring log fire. Galena took me to a restaurant and introduced me to the many writers and artists who were sitting there together on the long benches. The next day, she drove me back to my hotel in

Moscow where our perfect romantic idyll was somewhat marred by a fierce row that developed between Galena and the receptionist until the hotel agreed to give me a credit for my night away in the country.

And so began our liaison, that turned into a deep attachment after such an unpromising start. Galena and I found an apartment together in Moscow, which cost US$18,000. I decided against buying it as I was unsure then how the relationship would develop. Instead, I rented the apartment for US$800 a month. This proved to be a mistake. When we parted amicably three years later, she bought the apartment for the going price of US$80,000.

During our three years together, Galena worked as Marketing Director for a leading advertising agency, where she was very successful, although her volatile temperament led to many clashes with her staff.

Galena displayed another strong characteristic of the Russian woman. She could be unpredictable as well as reliable. If she felt loved by a man, she would do anything to support him; but, if she felt neglected or uncared for, she would drop him at once. There was no halfway situation.

Thanks to her, ITE was able to recruit some of the finest sales people that she screened individually and recommended. As my attractive escort, she was not only an eye-stopper but equally capable of networking socially among the powerful Russian elite. She introduced me to Moscow's dacha circuit on weekends to which foreigners rarely get invited, let alone allowed in. It was through some of these weekend invitations that I was able to obtain ministerial support for my projects.

On my first visit to Kiev, Edouard invited Vika (the girl friend whom he saw seldom, with a wealthy Georgian boyfriend) to meet him at the Kievskya Hotel. Vika brought her friend Taiya with her. Taiya was tall, thin and blonde – a typical Ukrainian beauty – with a thirteen-year-old daughter. I laid on dinner for all of them at the hotel restaurant, which boasted a floorshow.

It was still light at 7.00 pm when we sat down to the mini-banquet that I had ordered. Taiya was cold and distant, speaking little, even when I tried to make conversation with her. However, her behaviour was explained not just by her lack of English but also by the tragic death only six months earlier of her boyfriend Dimitri, a former KGB man who had been killed in a motorcar accident. Taiya had been devastated and our dinner was her first social outing since then, at the instigation of Vika, who persuaded her that she needed to get out of her apartment. There was no outcome that evening from our dinner meeting, but I left it that, if and when I returned to Kiev, I would look her up.

Taiya lived with her parents and her daughter in Boyurka, a suburb of Kiev about 20 minutes from the city centre. She had married when she was 21 and divorced at 26. A year later, she began to date Dimitri, who was himself married and worked for the KGB. Their affair lasted for seven years and, during the last two years, she lived with him. Taiya had her own career as a chief engineer in a forestry group but left her job when Dimitri died. By the time that I met her she was 34.

She had been unimpressed when I told her that I would call her from London. At that time she trusted nobody, especially foreigners. In fact, I was the first foreigner that she had met. Her friend Vika, who dated foreigners frequently, convinced her that they were not to be trusted and were only there to be used. As an example of the gulf between East and West, the common perception at that time in Kiev, and elsewhere, was that foreigners were there to be exploited and that 'locals' could make money from them, either through gifts or by being given help to secure a job. The corollary to this attitude was that, however generous foreigners might be, they could be neither believed nor trusted.

As a Westerner who was new to the East of Europe and not wise in its ways, my perception of relationships with girls like Taiya was equally cynical and unflattering. Girls like her would only want to go out with foreign strangers in order to extract money from them. I felt that the story about Dimitri had been fed to me in order to gain my sympathy so that I would be generous towards her. My impression was that Taiya could probably be easily bought, particularly since she was a friend of Vika, who 'traded in' foreigners faster than anyone else and had managed to use them to secure seven flats, a motorcar and Western clothes in just under a year.

In short, I was ready to condemn poor Taiya as guilty by association. In fact, as events were to show, I was completely wrong in my initial judgement about her. The impression that Russian and Ukrainian women were 'loose' was, in most cases, a misconception. They were genuinely friendly rather than promiscuous. They had a natural *joie de vivre*, loved life to the full and were happy just to eat, laugh and, sometimes, make love.

I had no time to go shopping before I left for London but I gave Taiya US$100 as a present for her daughter. She didn't understand why I was doing this but accepted reluctantly – she clearly felt uncomfortable about it. Edouard thought I was being stupid in making a gift to Taiya, and told me so. According to Edouard, what I had done was contrary to 'his' Russian practice. Russian generosity began after a meal and spending the night with a girl, not before.

Three weeks later, I called Taiya from London to say that I would be visiting Kiev soon and wanted to see her again. It was early June when I returned and the city looked clean and beautiful in the spring sunshine. I went straight from the airport to a morning business meeting but my afternoon was free. Taiya and I joined Edouard, and the twins with whom he had taken up on the return trip from our first visit to Kiev, for lunch at a hotel. After lunch, while Edouard spent the afternoon enjoying himself with the twins, Taiya took me off to show me Kiev. We walked through the park for two hours before arriving at a more secluded area where there was a large, derelict building. I was mystified as she led me through a labyrinth of deserted rooms until we reached the place where she and Dimitiri had carved their names on a wooden post. This was the place where they had first fallen in love some seven years before. At this point, Taiya became upset and burst into tears. I waited patiently until her sobs subsided.

When it was time to return, we did not take a taxi but instead walked back across the park. Taiya looked beautiful and was relaxed as she took off her shoes to walk across the grass. We arrived back at the hotel at about 6.00 pm; I had to attend a business dinner but asked her if she would wait in my room so that we could have a drink together afterwards. She agreed, with the assurance that I would pay for her taxi home. Travelling on the Metro late at night was unsafe, as was the half-hour walk she would have had to take from the station.

After the dinner, Edouard wanted to talk business, but all that I wanted to do was to have a quiet drink with Taiya and pleaded tiredness. I arrived back at my room at 9.30 pm and spent an enjoyable and companionable hour with Taiya before putting her into a taxi, where we parted with a friendly kiss. On the way back to my room I encountered Edouard, who told me that I was acting like a fool. Taiya was a nothing, he said, and I should not take her seriously. 'In Russia,' he told me 'we just make love to women and I don't give them any importance.' I detected that Edouard was also annoyed, perhaps jealous, that Taiya had taken precedence over business. And, when he found out that nothing had happened between us, he added that there were so many women out there, why would I waste time on one that wouldn't go to bed with me?

The following day, on returning from a meeting at lunchtime, I found Taiya waiting for me in the hotel lobby. She suggested that we skip lunch and go for a swim in the Kiev river, which was very warm for early June. She looked gorgeous in her bikini and I could hardly believe my eyes. After swimming, we went back to the hotel and hugged. Taiya was gentle and caring and seemed very natural and genuine – far from the image of a person who made a habit of sleeping with as many foreign men as possible. I tried to give her a present, but she didn't want one.

As I have related, Edouard and I did manage to book space for the 1st Kiev International Motor Show and Taiya kept me informed of developments while I was away from Kiev. It was unfortunate that taking help from someone else caused problems with Edouard who became jealous.

As my relationship with Taiya developed, she introduced me to her mother, father, daughter and sister. Now in retirement, her father was sharing his house with four women. They had little money but formed a very nice, close-knit and friendly family. The late lunch that they gave me was very special and must have cost them a month's savings. While they were very proud to be entertaining me, they did not want their neighbours to know that there was a foreigner in their house; so, they drew the curtains, made music and we sang songs. I noticed that they had no television and the next day had one delivered with a thank-you note saying that I looked forward to seeing them again in the future.

I made many visits to Kiev and our friendship continued to grow. At all times, I was completely honest with her, making it plain that not only was I separated but that I was also involved with another woman as well.

Before the Motor Show was staged, Taiya announced that she had quit her present job and would like to work for the company if there was an opening. If she joined the company she could feed back information and protect my interests. I thought that it was an excellent idea and engaged her.

From Taiya I learned how family-oriented Ukrainian women are. If you help look after her and her family, she'll look after you. This was contrary to the perception of the majority of macho Russian men who were convinced that the only way to keep their women was with money alone. On several occasions I invited Taiya to London and took her, along with her sister and daughter, on holidays abroad. She was very appreciative and, with my encouragement, decided to focus on bringing up her daughter and not to pursue the idea of a full-time relationship with me. However, we kept in touch and continued to meet from time to time. She expected nothing more from me, and we remained good friends. As previously described, ITE staged four or five exhibitions in Kiev before deciding to pull out after the 1st Kiev International Motor Show.

Taiya later joined an international investment bank as Promotions Manager at the company's head office, where she is now in charge of the advertising department.

Irina was a project manager at an Exhibition Centre in St Petersburg, who happened to be attending a meeting of ITE personnel in Cyprus. She had an excellent job, was married to a banker and had a wonderful son studying in England. We met in Cyprus where there was a meeting of minds but nothing more happened.

Some time later, Irina visited England and I located a job for her son. At the end of her six-day visit, she suggested that we should go somewhere and celebrate before her return flight to St Petersburg. She wanted some way to repay me for the kindness that I had shown her.

Irina asked me if we could go for lunch to Cliveden, the old Astor family home now converted to a hotel, before driving on to Heathrow Airport to catch her evening flight. She was quite taken aback by the beauty of Cliveden and we took a boat out onto the lake and talked about everything under the sun. When we returned to the hotel, I asked if we could hire a room for Irina to change in before setting out for the airport but was told that it was fully booked. Fortunately I had a friend who knew the Cliveden manager's wife, and we managed to inveigle the use of a room up to 6.00 pm.

The room was magnificent and the furnishings included a tapestry-hung four-poster bed. While Irina went to the bathroom to freshen up and change, I lay down on the bed and, fatigued by my unaccustomed exercise as a boatman, fell asleep. When I awoke, I found that Irina had washed but not changed and was lying next to me on the bed. She moved towards me and we slept in each other's arms.

On the way to the airport, we agreed that what had happened should be kept secret and that no one else should ever know. We became firm friends and saw each other many more times but there were no further intimate occasions.

As a good friend, Irina proved very helpful to ITE's expansion in St Petersburg. Among other things she was the first to tip me off about Sergei, who had been her close associate and, within five years, was to become ITE's principal partner in Russia.

You can't win them all. Svetlana was the Deputy Manager of a Sports Palace in Moscow. She was an independent, happily married businesswoman. She was also tough and had survived for the last 20 years of the communist era while other directors came and went. She was sporty – a keen skier and swimmer, and a beautiful, seductive woman; she led me on but never let me succeed.

Svetlana visited London for an ITE business meeting. After three days' work, I took her to see *Phantom of the Opera* – the current leading hit musical in town. Unfortunately, everyone who came to London from abroad wanted to see it, and I had sat through it many times. It didn't take long after we took our seats in the stalls and the lights dimmed for me to fall asleep. Perversely, Svetlana found this social lapse endearing and was quite turned on by it. After the show, now wide awake and refreshed, I took a rather tired Svetlana to Joe Allen's to eat. I was able to point out to her the various actors and actresses dining there that night and we talked about everything except business.

We arrived back at Svetlana's hotel at about 1.30 am I suggested that we should go to her room for a nightcap but Svetlana firmly refused. Feeling too tired to go home, I booked myself into a room but sleep wouldn't come because I couldn't stop thinking about Svetlana. At 3.00 am I rang her room and asked if I could come over as I had something very urgent to discuss.

Svetlana let me in and we made, as they say, mad passionate love.

This was the first time in my life that I felt somehow that it was I who was being used. When we had finished, Svetlana stated that she did not want anyone to know what had happened.

The next day Svetlana missed her business meetings, using a shopping trip as her excuse. Back in Moscow, I never saw her again. At subsequent meetings with the Sports Palace, Svetlana was always represented by assistants and never attended in person. Unfortunately, this brief fling made our deteriorating relations with the Sports Palace much worse, not better.

Edouard's best friend had a daughter, called Anaied, who had recently graduated from university. He asked me if the girl could come and stay with me in London for a month to study English. I met the father, mother and daughter in Edouard's office and agreed to Anaeid staying with me at my London home during August. The parents were worried because the girl had never been outside Russia before and were concerned that something might happen to her. Anaeid asked if she could bring a friend with her, called Galena, who was the daughter of another exhibition partner and who also wanted to study English. Accepting the logic that there might be safety in numbers and that the presence of a friend might relieve the burden of entertainment, I agreed.

Anaeid's mother, Tamara, had been a schoolteacher but was now engaged in real estate with her brother. When I met her she looked so young that I could not believe that she had a grown-up daughter. I organized visas and made the necessary travel arrangements for the two girls, but Tamara was still concerned whether I could look after her daughter when she was in England. She gave me a box of chocolates as a present before leaving.

At dinner with Edouard, I asked him to tell me what he knew about Tamara. It turned out that she and Anaeid's father were divorced and had only got together for their meeting with me. I asked Edouard if he thought I could invite Tamara out but Edouard said definitely not. He had known Tamara for 20 years and she was not the type to go out at the drop of a hat.

The two girls arrived in London and at first things did not go well. They were very untidy, left their room in a complete mess, wouldn't talk to or even acknowledge the staff at our large house in St John's Wood and would not eat the food put in front of them. They were late getting up in the morning – I had planned to take them with me to the office for three hours each day before they went to language school – and didn't seem to bathe very often. A member of my office staff took one of the girls out to a bar and asked her what she wanted to drink. He told me how much he was taken aback when she asked for champagne (it emerged later that she had seen a similar scene in a movie and really had no idea what to ask for).

This was the last straw and I had had enough. I telephoned Edouard and told him that I was not a nanny and wanted to get rid of the girls and to put them up in a hotel. I asked him to call Anaeid's mother to explain the situation. The upshot was that Tamara called Anaeid and shouted at her, demanding to know what was going on. Then the truth emerged. Both girls, it seemed, believed that they should do as little as possible to disturb the peace of their hosts, including not bathing in the morning or evening, because the filling water tanks would make a noise, nor eating too much. Once the 'misunderstanding' on both sides was cleared, things started to improve.

A transformation in behaviour occurred. From then on, both girls were washed and ready at 8.00 am, had breakfasted by 8.15 and were ready to leave with me at 8.30 for the office. They tidied their room, kept it in an immaculate state, bought flowers for their hostess, left notes whenever they went out and, in the end turned out to be wonderful kids.

While Anaeid and Galena were in London I had not thought further about Tamara, but when I returned to Moscow for the next Motor Show that autumn, Tamara invited Edouard and me to dinner to thank us for looking after the girls. That evening Tamara looked fabulous. I told her that I knew she was divorced and asked her if she would like to go out with me.

She was unsure.

I had Tamara's telephone number and called her several times. She was intrigued by my insistence but still not sure whether or not to go out with me. I discovered that she was seeing the Head of a TV Network at the time and was also focusing on her career in real estate. I continued to invite Tamara for dinner and she continued to decline. Finally, she agreed to meet me for lunch. We met and chatted easily; I had brought along photographs of the girls in London and we talked about what had happened with them. With lunch over, I asked if she would join me for dinner. She agreed but only if her old friend Edouard was present.

I instructed Edouard that he should turn up for dinner but, at the earliest opportunity, should make his excuses and take his leave. Edouard duly did what was expected of him, but when he got up to leave Tamara asked for a lift home. Thinking on his feet, Edouard said that he was going in the wrong direction. Tamara agreed to stay, on the condition that I arranged a taxi for her later.

Once alone, I admitted to Tamara that she had been constantly in my thoughts and how much I wanted to see her. Would she give me a chance? She was divorced and I was recently separated. Tamara stopped eating but smiled. She had heard a lot about me, most of which was not good. My reputation was that of a *babnik* or flirt and she felt that I was 'above' her and used my 'superiority' to seduce all the women I met.

There was no point in protesting and I decided that I had to take a chance myself. I told Tamara that I had been waiting a long time for this moment, and just wanted her to give me a chance so that she could get to know me. She replied that she was not sure about starting another relationship; she saw her present companion just twice a month and it was only eight months since she had divorced her husband, after 17 years of marriage.

I asked her straight out if she would spend the evening with me, arguing that if it didn't work out we could part, having just enjoyed some fun together. Then I took her by the hand and led her to the roof of the hotel where I told her that this was our night and that we should give each other a chance. Tamara was taken by surprise and allowed me to take her to my room. Although it was not an earthshaking experience for either of us, it was as if we had known each other for years. Afterwards, as I told her about my years as an inventor, we laughed and joked so much that it was better than the act of love itself.

Tamara invited Edouard and I for dinner at her home and I asked him not to turn up. I was very tired that evening after a full day's work. Tamara gave me a lavish dinner, complete with vodka, after which I sat in front of the TV and fell asleep, not awaking until after 1.00 am. I wanted to return to my hotel so that I could be ready for my first meeting in the morning so Tamara flagged down a taxi to take me back.

Tamara's dinner had been on a Thursday night and I was due to leave for London on the Saturday following. We met again before I left and I invited her to come to Antalya in Turkey for an ITE meeting in three weeks' time. Tamara said that she would think about it but that she would not come unless she could arrive five days before the conference and leave before the delegates arrived. By this time we were already close and I asked her not to go back to her man but to give me a chance of building a serious relationship with her.

Eventually, Tamara agreed to come to Anatlya, where we got to know each other much better away from the pressures of Moscow. She explained to me how unhappy she had been in her marriage but that she had been unable to leave her husband at the time because of the high standard of living they enjoyed as a result of his top job in the Russian theatre. Following *perestroika,* he had been reluctant to adjust to changing times and she had at last found the freedom to leave him. After our four days in Turkey together, Tamara went back to Moscow and told her man that she would not be seeing him again.

Tamara and I grew increasingly close. She found a flat for me to live in when I was in Moscow. Initially, she didn't want me to live in her own flat but the following year, as our relationship deepened and we became confident of its permanence, Tamara used her real estate expertise to find a large flat for the two of us to live together. We stayed there for five years, before moving to the dacha some 40 minutes outside Moscow, where we live now.

By now, I realized that ITE's near-monopoly of the Moscow exhibition scene had become too prominent and an anomaly. I felt sure that it would not be long before it became a target for the big Russian groups. My stable relationship with Tamara also contributed to a change in my personal sense of direction. We decided to take ITE public so that I could cash in my investment as a stepping stone to getting out of the company. Now I could hope to settle down to live a normal life.

Chapter 10

ITE Comes of Age

ITE's activities had grown from one exhibition in one city to 70 exhibitions in 18 cities, covering some 15 countries. Our Moscow office grew geometrically in staff numbers as we expanded and now employed more than 300. Overall, ITE employed 453 people worldwide. Communications were maintained and systems administered through computer installations. Specialist staff were recruited to prepare the company for a Stock Exchange listing from 1997 onwards.

With the burden of ITE's day-to-day operations having shifted to Mark Webber and Mark Shashoua, Roddy and I were able to focus more on the long-range planning of the company. Reviewing our forward outlook, we had two major strategic concerns. The first was that ITE had become too visible in Moscow and was therefore potentially vulnerable as a possible target for the Russian groups. Through its organization of over 30 trade fairs and the immensely popular Moscow International Motor and Tourism shows, ITE had become a household name and could be a target because it was perceived in some quarters as being a cash cow that generated millions in hard currency. The reality was somewhat different. While ITE had a healthy turnover and made a profit, it paid taxes in both the UK and Russia. Its accounting and banking arrangements were entirely transparent and correct. ITE owed its success to having been in the right place at the right time.

For advice on how to address this threat, I consulted with our consultant Alex who had worked for us so effectively in solving our early problems in Almaty with the Kazakhstan Oil and Gas Show. Alex's solution to the Moscow threat required a difficult decision. He advised that the only way for ITE to consolidate and expand in Russia was to leave and hand over control of the exhibitions to Russians in a Russian company, which he offered to head up as chairman. ITE in London would then organize the international side of the exhibitions and the Russian company would organize the Russian side. Reluctantly, we accepted the logic of this proposal, made an agreement with Alex for 15 years and handed over the Russian arm of ITE into Russian control. This draconian restructure ensured that ITE and its achievements would not disintegrate.

About this time I became aware of an upcoming new star in the Russian exhibitions firmament. His name was Sergei and he had come from nowhere to set up and run 38 exhibitions. Sergei was young and dynamic, a nationalist and former communist who had previously worked as Deputy Director at LenExpo in St Petersburg. He believed strongly that exhibitions in Russia should be run by Russian companies and not foreigners and attributed the successes of ITE to the market void that ITE had filled, enabling them to carve out their market leading shares. After leaving LenExpo, Sergei set up his first 24 exhibitions in St Petersburg without any financial support. I immediately recognized Sergei as a powerful threat, although my advisers did not, and foresaw that he would soon be moving into Moscow. My fears were reinforced by Edouard's opinion that although Sergei was an unknown upstart he was obviously skilled and talented and very much a rising nationalistic force.

I decided to ask Sergei if we could meet on the pretext that, since he was running a Tourism Show in St Petersburg and ITE had announced that it would also be staging a tourism exhibition there, perhaps we could find a way to avoid a clash. Initially it was difficult to make contact, but eventually Sergei agreed to meet me at a hotel. I wanted to size up our new opposition and had in mind that we could either buy his show or enter into a partnership.

At the hotel, I found that Sergei spoke little but was highly focused and, when he did speak, he made sure that every word was significant. I opened the discussion by asking Sergei why he was competing with ITE by staging a tourism show in St Petersburg. Sergei's reply was simple: 'Your facts are not correct.' Two years before, Sergei had visited London and contacted ITE to ask if we would be interested in co-operating in a tourism show in St Petersburg. No one had informed me of this approach and two weeks later he had received a letter from an ITE staff member telling him, short-sightedly, that ITE had no interest in his proposal. Accordingly, Sergei approached Reed, another leading British exhibition company, and asked them to be partners in his tourism show – an invitation which they accepted. The reason why he had agreed to meet me now was to ensure that I would abort the ITE show. His case was that Reed had got there first and should therefore be left alone to get on with its show (or else!)

In response, I expressed my surprise that Reed had agreed to do business with Sergei since he was an unknown; in the past, ironically, Reed had refused to work with ITE. I asked him what was the scope of the agreement that he had signed with Reed and Sergei told me that he had only agreed to co-operate on the tourism show. The rest of his themes were open to discussion. I began to think that ITE would have to pull out and cancel its St Petersburg Tourism Show and apologized to Sergei for the way that he had been treated by ITE two years previously. I then asked if he would like to co-operate with ITE on future themes in St Petersburg. He replied that he would think about it.

He gave me a lift back to my hotel. Although he had been courteous and fair, the meeting had confirmed all that I had feared as to the serious nature of the threat he posed to ITE. As he opened the car door, Sergei looked me in the eye and said that he hoped I had decided to cancel ITE's Tourism Show in St Petersburg. I asked him if he could give me a face-saving formula that I could use to explain to my staff why I was cancelling. Sergei understood my predicament and said that he would be in touch, although he couldn't promise anything.

Three days later, I received a call from Reed Exhibitions saying that since ITE had withdrawn from St Petersburg, would it be possible to reach an agreement over future exhibitions? As a result, ITE and Reed signed a reciprocal agreement in which ITE undertook for 50 years not to stage a tourism show in St Petersburg, and Reed undertook, for the same period, not to go to Moscow. Having signed the agreement, I telephoned Sergei and congratulated him on beating ITE. In response, Sergei suggested that he would like to do business with ITE on other themes. I realized then that ITE had lost one show but, by being honest, had probably gained 20 others. Into the bargain, ITE later managed to 'poach' one of Reed Elsevier's main board directors as a member of ITE's Board of Directors – an achievement that certainly impressed Sergei.

On further reflection, I felt that Sergei would prove to be a great asset to ITE. He was a true patriot who wanted to do his best for Russia as well as for himself. On the one hand, I knew that I could help him to achieve his goals; on the other, I understood that in the long run I would be better off helping Sergei rather than hindering him. We soon reached an agreement on other themes. My friendship with Sergei flourishes to this day and, as I predicted, Sergei has now become one of Russia's most influential players in the media field.

★

My second major concern at this stage was that, geographically speaking, we had put all our eggs into the single basket of Russia and the CIS. I began to feel that it would be wise to hedge our bets and perhaps lay the groundwork for our next venture, if and when we decided to cash in by taking ITE public.

I had always been fascinated by India. With its 1-billion-plus population, it was analogous to China and reminded me of the lost opportunity there. If we were to look for challenges beyond Europe, why not India? Roddy was not at all interested and I decided to pay a visit to India on my own to carry out a personal fact-finding mission.

After landing in New Delhi, I began to investigate the state of the Indian trade fair industry which, at that time, was controlled by the government. No private shows were allowed without the sanction of the ministry. I found that bribery was pervasive in everyday affairs and there was no opportunity to achieve anything without an Indian partner.

It was very clear to me that if Russia was risky, India was an even higher risk. Behind the gentle, anglophile approach of the Indian businessman lay many treacherous problems into which one would inevitably be drawn. The risk-reward ratio was definitely tilted in favour of the Indian partner. Nevertheless, if only to satisfy my curiosity, I decided to test out four expositions there: a Delhi Oil and Gas Show, a Medical Show, a Construction Show and, last but not least, a Delhi Fashion Show.

The experience convinced me of India's undoubted potential but, at that time in 1996, it was no Russia or China. Exploiting the business opportunity would be a slow process, but the future opening up of the market under a system of government that was, in reality, more akin to Russian neo-socialism than democracy gave the promise of an ultimate goldmine. Today in 2007, with GDP growth in excess of 9 per cent and the opening of its financial markets, the Indian promise is being fulfilled.

★

Back in Moscow, Edouard had suggested further expansion into the CIS Republic and ITE decided to enter Turkmenistan and stage an Oil and Gas Show. The show was opened by Saparmurat Niyazov, Turkmenistan's President and by the President of Gazprom, Moscow, an important milestone in the history of ITE's Oil and Gas Shows. Previously, Gazprom had been precluded from participating in any of ITE's shows under an agreement with Germany's Ruhrgas, which banned it from taking part in any ITE British organized show in Russia.

In the meantime, the Moscow office, under the direction of Alex, pushed the expansion of exhibitions organized by the Russian arm of ITE into other regions of Russia: Nizny Novgorod, Samara and Rostov on Don. This extension of activities within Mother Russia brought the total number of exhibitions organized by ITE up to 100, covering 22 themes or product categories in 18 cities in Russia and the CIS.

The exiled Mikhail wanted to expand the business that he was growing for ITE in Bahrain. Because the country was so small, he looked to the Kingdom of Saudi Arabia – the largest and most economically powerful oil-rich country in the Arab world. With the help of his Bahraini team, he was able to organize SAUDIO-PEC, the Saudi International Oil Exhibition in Dammam. At the same time, our Indian counterpart with whom we had co-operated succeeded in winning permission to stage the Delhi International Oil and Gas Show, together with an accompanying conference, to be followed by a Delhi International Medical Show, Delhi Construction Show and Delhi Jewellery Show.

ITE reached its peak in 1998. Each division was self-perpetuating through the geographical cloning of successful exhibition titles licensed from Blenheim, and could continue to achieve 30–40 per cent cumulative annual growth. The further way forward required a change of direction. Instead of ITE organizing shows itself, I felt that we should look for aspiring entrepreneurs like Sergei to take over the organization role. Relations with ExpoCentre were improving and VDNK were becoming stronger by the day. Our market share in St Petersburg and Kazakhstan had reached an all-time high. The annual number of visitors to ITE shows reached 3 million, with 9,500 corporate exhibitors participating at some 100 trade events.

With ITE sales surpassing the US$80 million mark and pre-tax profits nearing US$20 million, we felt the need to enlarge the board in preparation for the listing of the company's shares on the AIM market of the London Stock Exchange. We recruited Sir Hugh Bidwell, the former Lord Mayor of the City of London; Hugh Beaver, a prominent City figure; Mr Ian Thomas, a main board member of the Reed Elsevier organization, plus a senior partner of the 'Big Three' international accountancy firm Coopers & Lybrand as non-executive directors to help guide ITE to even greater success in the future.

The preparations for going public in 1998 took up much of our time. With operations in 12 countries, 20 joint ventures and many complex commercial agreements, the certification of our books and the due diligence process was a costly nightmare. However, the promise of 1,000 times the US$100,000 investment made in 1991 kept us going. In March 1998, ITE was voted Europe's fastest growing medium-sized company by *Business Week* magazine and the four of us – Roddy, both Marks and I, were also voted top entrepreneurs of that year in a subsequent *Business Week* survey.

We were among the first companies doing business in Russia to float on the London Stock Exchange also receiving the 'Queen's Award for Export'. Now in 2007, dozens if not hundreds of Russian companies are listing their shares on stock exchanges including Gazprom and the 2006 listing of Rosneft in an independent public offering (IPO) worth US$11 billion. What a remarkable change in just eight years. As an indication of the progress that the Russian economy has made in the interval, Russia now has foreign exchange reserves of more than US$200 billion, compared with the deficit of US$30 billion when the World Bank bailed it out in 1998 with a much needed US$2 billion loan.

As soon as we let it be known that we were preparing for an IPO, we were hounded by private equity funds, investment bankers and all kinds of financial advisers, with a variety of proposals as to how we could keep ITE private. All of these proposals involved accepting a lesser capitalization multiple than we could achieve through an IPO but with the promise of even more riches after another five-year run. 'Why do you need money?' was their unanimous, resounding message. 'You and Roddy already take annual dividends of over US$4 million each; you can go public later.'

There followed a sterile dialogue with the venture capitalists to whom we put the reciprocal question: 'If we don't need the money now, why do we need you?' 'To expand' was their response but the answer was not convincing. We were already growing at a phenomenal rate; the cost of four years or more of expansion would mean more investment in infrastructure and more exposure to our uncertain markets. We had enjoyed a good run of seven years. Having survived the Russian Financial Crisis of 1998, who knew what might happen in Russia next?

The period of the 1998 financial crisis in Russia was one of stress and uncertainty, from which ITE fortunately emerged unscathed. All banks in Moscow closed their doors, all deposits were frozen, cash machines were blocked and no withdrawals were permitted. People and businesses functioned only in cash and in dollars. The rouble collapsed and Russian bonds, losing practically all their value, became worthless. The Moscow Stock Market fell sharply and the only bank that operated was SBER Bank, which is state-owned. The ensuing consolidation through closures and mergers resulted in the disappearance of at least 40 per cent of the small Russian banks.

However, one personal experience suggested that all was not quite as it seemed. I had opened an account at AutoBank, on the recommendation of a local joint venture colleague, to which I transferred US$50,000, with the intention of buying a motorcar for a Russian girl whose company I had enjoyed. When the crisis hit, the bank closed its doors at all branches and blocked all withdrawals and deposits at its Moscow branches. I called my colleague to tell him that my deposit was frozen and that my girlfriend wanted her car, crisis or no crisis, which I was due to purchase for her at the Moscow Motor Show in two weeks' time. My friend took the news calmly. 'At which branch did you deposit your money, and what was the account number?' he asked me. I told him and 20 minutes later he called me back. 'Roger, your money is already back in your account in London. I told you that it was a safe bank.' I called my bank and, sure enough, the money transfer had just arrived. The incident confirmed my suspicion that some Russian banks were not as badly off as reported. In fact, they had exaggerated the banking crisis in order to gain market share in the sector.

ITE survived the crisis because international companies felt safe exhibiting with a foreign-controlled company. In the event of cancellation, it was the best capitalized company in its field in Russia and could withstand the crisis, which it did. In fact, our business grew by 30 per cent during the period of the crisis until the situation returned to normal.

While we were deliberating the question of flotation, I received a telephone call from a Monaco-based businessman called Lawrie Lewis who had been one of the two founders of the Blenheim Group, which had evolved into a public company. Blenheim went on through acquisitions to become one of Europe's leading trade fair companies. He stated that he had a proposition to put to us. I was intrigued by Lawrie Lewis's story, which seemed relevant to our situation, and persuaded Roddy that we should at least meet him to learn the lessons of his past experience and how he felt now having sold out previously.

On the occasion of our first meeting Lawrie came alone and our meeting was both cordial and entertaining. He was a most amusing man, but his intentions were serious. He explained that he was bored, having cashed in his shareholding in Blenheim in its early years and was frustrated to have seen it grow into a great company. He would like to be business active again. He proposed to us what we felt could be the best of both worlds. An offer to take ITE public through the reverse takeover of a public company vehicle that he controlled, together with a guarantee that the founder shareholders – Roddy and I – would receive the equivalent of US$100 million. His proposal was straightforward: if we accepted the offer in principle he would consult with his bankers, Investec, and if their response was favourable the deal would be on; if not, the deal would be off. In any event, either party would have the opportunity to withdraw if it was not satisfied.

We could see little risk in testing Lawrie's offer and allocated a period of three months to check it out. It was the only offer on the table that valued ITE at US$130 million plus approximately US$16 million cash in the company. After further discussions we agreed to sell part of our founders' shares, thereby realising US$80 million.

Investec as the public company's broker agreed to the planned share offering via a reverse takeover and to place the shares as the company's broker in the market. Both Roddy and I were amazed by the positive market reception and we all decided that the transaction should go ahead on the understanding that I would remain Chairman for one year and that Laurie Lewis would be appointed CEO.

After twelve months, when I resigned, my son Mark, who was running the day-to-day operations, would become CEO and Lawrie would step up to be Chairman of the Group. Roddy decided to retire to Marbella and Miami with US$40 million, plus all the millions in dividends that he had accumulated over the years.

Having underwritten part of the share offering, Lawrie wanted to play an active role and immediately concentrated on making acquisitions rather than on the organic growth of the company. Inspired by Neville Buch's success in selling Blenheim for more than £540 million in 1998/9, Lawrie wanted to convert ITE into an even greater company.

As in all cases of differing management styles, friction soon arose when Lawrie started to replace management with appointees of his own choice.

These symptoms of disharmony were to be expected but not so early in the game. Mark was unhappy, although Lawrie could not have been more supportive of him. The truth was that Lawrie's management style worked for him but not for the Shashoua family, who still owned 25 per cent of the share capital. It was only a matter of time before Roddy and I sold our remaining shareholding for US$40 million, at which point Mark and I resigned.

Now in full control, Lawrie invited Veronis Suhler Media Fund (who had previously approached us to invest but had missed the opportunity) to invest US$60 million in the Group. This gave the company a war chest for acquisitions and it made its his first large acquisition – a Turkish trade fair company that was a leading venue organizer in Turkey. More acquisitions followed but the earthquake in Turkey seriously affected ITE, although only for a short period of time.

Lawrie also persuaded United News and Media to purchase 5 per cent of ITE as a show of confidence. Subsequently, the share price rebounded and, for a time, everything was rosy once more.

After a series of different managing directors had come and gone, the company decided that it was time for a change of direction. The venture capitalists with big shareholdings in ITE, such as Veronis Suhler, together with other members of the board and certain institutional shareholders allowed a former finance director under the Shashoua regime to take over as CEO. He concentrated on the company's core business in Russia and the CIS and, within a few years, ITE was back in the limelight.

By May 2007, ITE had reached a market value of almost US$1 billion, close to the valuation of Blenheim, when it was eventually sold out. Lawrie Lewis's judgement that one day ITE would achieve such heights and possibly surpass Blenheim in value at the time of Neville Buch's sell-out had been vindicated.

Did we decide to sell out too soon? Perhaps the decision was a poor one but, in hindsight, the exposure that we were getting in Russia in 1998 was at an all-time high, certainly in the view of all the large Russian groups who wondered how this little British company from nowhere had grown to become Russia's largest trade fair and events organizer. In fact, a consortium of Russian organizations was formed to do battle against the foreign organizations operating in Russia by lobbying for legislation to control trade fair activity and to take over the foreign organizers.

In 1998, we were expanding rapidly by adding new themes but we had no long tenures at any of the venues. The only feature of our insecure arrangements that seemed to save us was that the total annual value of rentals paid to the various venues had mounted close to US$10 million. In retrospect, that sum would have enabled us to own our own venues by purchasing land for US$4 to 5 million and erecting one or two exhibition halls of 20,000 square metres, each at a total cost of US$20–30 million. We would then have been self-sufficient. However, that was not to be, as it would have entailed the company investing a substantial amount of its reserves soon after surviving Russia's financial crisis and delay in cashing in on our investment.

The arithmetic was easy and the choice for us was made even easier; US$130 million in the pocket today was better than US$400 million in five years' time. Entrepreneurs are risk-takers with some degree of control over the fate of their enterprises, but gamblers we were not and we sold with a clear conscience. Another important consideration was that neither Roddy nor I possessed the management ability to really grow the Group to the heights for which we believed it was destined. 'You don't even know how to use a computer and you still think you can do it?' was Roddy's verdict, putting the final nail in the coffin of our decision-making. There really was no answer to that.

Selling out meant that our Russian partners could also cash in. They had not understood that the shares in their companies had an intrinsic value. For them, what was in their pockets gave value to their shares and enhanced their prestige. Managers who at the start were making US$200–400 a month were now making US$10,000–20,000 a month, still a pittance of course compared to the growing number of Russian millionaires. Our sell-out provided the basis of a valuation for the shares in the Russian companies of our partners to whom we had outsourced some of ITE's activities. Subsequently, they sold out too for more than US$20 million and their companies continued to grow alongside ITE; some have a value today in excess of US$300 million. Other directors and management employees of ITE shared over US$10 million in bonus payments, resulting from the sale of their share options in the company.

What an anti-climax I felt having sold out of ITE. Leaving the company was a more emotional experience for me than for Roddy. We were ready to sell but not ready for the future. Like a divorced woman or a rich widow, I was alone in London, lost and at sea. The price of my long absences in pursuit of a livelihood and my ambitions had sadly been the end of my marriage. If I had not chosen to work in Moscow and other dangerous places, or my wife had agreed to accompany me, perhaps we would have stayed together. Instead, we agreed to separate amicably.

I travelled and took an extended holiday but I missed the buzz of the motor shows and the company of my friends in Russia. My telephone was suddenly silent, I became irritable and for no logical reason I experienced stress attacks doing absolutely nothing.

Chapter 11

Getting it right:
The Expomedia Formula

Living in London after the decision to sell out the rest of my ITE shares and leave the company was an unfamiliar and new experience for me. Following an amicable parting with my wife, I sold our house in St John's Wood that I had bought only two years earlier, and moved to Chelsea, where I rented a small flat of 800 square-feet while looking for somewhere more permanent. I was keenly aware of the paradox between having gained a fortune and living alone in a tiny flat as a replacement for the beautiful US$6 million 5,000-square-foot contemporary home I had given up.

My brother Roddy – who shared equally in the sale of the ITE shares – had retired partly to Marbella having bought a magnificent yacht and penthouse a year earlier. He was now in the process of buying his second boat for use in Miami where he has been spending his winters. Roddy had found contentment and was enjoying life to the full. More recently, in 2003, we purchased two adjoining penthouses in the King's Chelsea Complex, London, which he visits occasionally.

Soon after moving, I received a call from my real estate representative who had located for me a lovely four-bedroom mews home that would serve admirably as my home base where I could write novels and collect art. After all, these are the pastimes for which Chelsea is famed. Every morning, I walked my local high street, the Fulham Road, getting to know most of the shop owners, restauranteurs and a few of the popular pubs.

However, it was not long before I was back in business of a sort, this time by chance. I needed somewhere to park my car and noticed a church right by my house with a vast empty car park that I began to use without asking permission. Some time after, I was accosted in my new-found car park by Jan, a well-known animator, who had achieved Hollywood fame with several movies such as *Freddy the Frog*, *Freddy Goes to Washington* and *Nelly the Dinosaur*. I had met Jan by accident earlier that year on a flight from London to Nice during the Cannes Film Festival. Both Roddy and I were on the flight but seated apart, as the flight was sold out. I ended up sitting next to Jan and inadvertently slept throughout the flight with my head having dropped sideways on to his shoulder. By the time we landed we had become firm friends.

'Is that your car parked by the church?' he asked me. I confirmed that it was indeed mine and he went on to tell me that the church was on lease to him for two years. He had offered the Church Commissioners to refurbish the church and restore it to its former glory. On completion of the improvements, his lease would be extended to 10 years and he would be free to use the premises as his animation studio, where he envisaged that over 100 animators would congregate to make further films of that genre for Hollywood studios.

Inspired by his enthusiasm and commitment, I began to feel alive for the first time in months and proposed to Jan that we put together a bid ourselves for the freehold of the property in order to justify the investment outlay of the considerable sums needed to restore and remodel the church. Local research revealed that a huge construction company, Bouygues France, was engaged in a £200-million project to develop apartments on adjacent properties of which they had acquired the freehold from the same principals, the Church Commissioners.

Using the approach that we intended to establish a cultural centre in Chelsea and should be given the opportunity to purchase the freehold, we opened protracted negotiations with the Church Commissioners. One year later, we were successful in purchasing the freehold for US$4 million, a firesale price. It was also certainly less than 20 per cent of the market value, considering that the church consisted of a building of over 15,000 square feet and a parking lot with space for more than 100 cars in the heart of Chelsea.

Having purchased the freehold and procured the necessary planning consents, we quickly converted the building into an office block with four floors, of which two floors each were assigned to Jan and myself. In return for the provision of the loan to purchase the building and refurbish, it was agreed that my two floors were rent-free and that, subject to planning permission on part of the parking lot either side of the former church, I could develop an office block and a house for my use. Once the house and office block were built, we would divide the freehold interest so that I would retain them and Jan would retain ownership of the converted church.

The church was a vast and very imposing structure, providing an excellent image for any new business in which I might engage. My clients would be seriously impressed. The only problem was that I had no clients and, in truth, didn't even have a business. I had many ideas, but on what fields should I focus and which idea should I explore first?

I yearned to be back in the exhibition game, but just to organize a new show would be boring; besides, my agreement with ITE prohibited me from competing with my old company for two years. At that moment, this seemed an eternity. As I studied the alternatives, I noticed the growing importance of the Internet in all spheres of business and concluded that any new venture should include an Internet element. In the context of trade shows, I foresaw that in time, 'virtual shows' would supercede – if not replace – actual live shows. The other thought that kept nagging at me was how to resolve all the problems that organizers encountered in securing stable venues. 'Why not own the venues?' presented itself as the ultimate solution. This idea intrigued me and continued to circulate in my mind.

In order to research both these notions I reverted to a study of the trade publications ranging across the exhibitions field, only to find that there was not one journal truly devoted to the field of exhibitions. In other fields there were hundreds of titles available to the interested reader. Perhaps I had discovered a gap in the market which could be filled by a useful magazine that would further new ideas and developments in the exhibitions industry.

I met Peter le Voir, who was also about to launch a new career – in his case in the venture capital field – to fund new companies with good ideas that he could back financially and in which he could become actively involved. He had the drive and initiative to strike out on his own rather than work for any of the big private equity funds. Peter was an excellent and experienced manager and financial analyst – just the man on whom to bounce off my ideas. After only a few discussions he came back to me with a business concept – 'Expomedia' – that incorporated all the elements on which I had been pondering.

Expomedia was conceived as the holding company for three separate activities: the ownership and operation of exhibition venues, an Internet division and a media division. While the development of the first two divisions was envisaged as organic growth activity, the media division would be grown by the acquisition of an existing core company.

The idea of building our own exhibition venues continued to evolve. An early decision was where to build our first centre. From our past experience and because Barbara Hanlon, who had left ITE after me, was Polish and supportive of the idea, we settled on Poland as our choice and proceeded to locate a site. To our amazement we discovered that owning a site in Poland was extremely expensive and that to actually build a centre was so capital intensive that we needed funding of at least US$20 million.

Financing was not available through banks because exhibition centres, unlike hotels or supermarkets, could not provide a key tenant with a reliable covenant. Exhibition organizers would only book or rent once they saw a completed centre and, even if they booked then, it would be for events a year later. In short, the task of financing a private exhibition centre fell straight back on our shoulders. Then we thought that if we were to build an events business that would eventually build up the centre, we could be 'the tenancy that the bank required' ourselves. However, this would be a Herculean task, to say the least, as we would need to launch a minimum of 20 events to satisfy this requirement. The development of such an events business would need at least US$2 million in working capital, despite our 30 years of experience in the field.

Peter's venture capital company had a limited budget, a far cry from the US$20 million plus required for the development of the centre alone. To add to the financial requirement, we estimated a minimum of US$1.5 million for development of the Internet division and all three divisions were classified as high risk since nobody in our field had tested the ideas previously.

For the next three months Peter and I researched the various ways in which we could strengthen our holding company. Finally we decided that, as the way forward, I would invest US$7.2 million, representing 60 per cent of the equity, and invite a major venture capital fund to put up finance of US$12.8 million for the 40 per cent balance of the equity. In discussion, Peter introduced us to Amro Ventures, based in Budapest, which liked our proposal because it fulfilled the three basic criteria that venture capitalists seek:

- Expomedia would fill a void in the market
- once successful, Expomedia could be the leading company in its field

- the former ITE management team of Darra Comyn, Constantine Bridgeman and Mark Shashoua were experienced with a good track record.

The evidence of ITE's track record was more than enough to satisfy all three criteria and Amro Ventures agreed to invest.

A private company, Expocentre Eastern Europe was formed to launch the Warsaw International Expocentre. Barely had the ink dried on our agreement than I began to consider how, if we were lucky and successful, we would be able to launch a chain of centres and become a truly billion-dollar company within five years. The corporate structure that we had put in place was fine for Warsaw but would not be suitable for a chain. Immediately, our thoughts turned to going public now rather than later, but in order to float, a three-year trading statement was required and our company was only a year old. The alternative was to buy a company with a clean, three-year track record into which we could reverse Expomedia.

Locating a site in Warsaw for our proposed exposition centre was not only a tragic-comical experience but also exposed me to the complicated way in which real estate was purchased in Poland and, in an even more convoluted way, how it could be developed. Although an independent state since the disintegration of the Soviet Union, Poland had still not changed the archaic legal system that it had inherited so as to accommodate the current avalanche of investments. Its laws were opaque, with many 'grey areas' and provided no protection for buyers of land. The concept of a 'clean title' was noticeably absent. No matter who bought a plot, one day the buyer could find the land confiscated if the courts ruled that the previous owner was someone other than the entity or person from whom it had been purchased.

The design and approval of architects' plans involved a maze of bureaucratic departments which were set up in command economy days for the sole purpose of creating jobs and generating opportunities for bribes at all levels, ensuring that permissions were granted. If you wish to succeed, adding 20 per cent to the cost of any project undertaken to cover unforeseen local expenses is a useful formula to follow.

After two weeks of searching, visits to the friends and acquaintances of our Russian contacts in Poland identified major real estate players in Warsaw who would be able to locate or procure for us a 2-hectare site for our proposed ExpoCentre, which we narrowed to a shortlist of two. After visiting the first of the shortlist I was depressed and ready to throw in the towel but then our contact introduced us to Janus, an experienced Warsaw developer who immediately understood what we wanted. Getting him to work with us was quite another matter, as his opening comments made clear: 'I'm No. 1 Polish developer – not interested in Mickey Hickey cash and I will build centre for you. If you accept, Janus finds plot for you. Also, I need confirmation you don't waste my time.'

As our relationship developed, we finally located a suitable site in the Wolla district of Warsaw, five minutes from the city centre, at a price of US$4 million for 2 hectares. We paid US$2 million to Janus to be his 50 per cent partner in the plot, on the understanding that once planning permission had been granted he would construct the centre.

At the time, we were unaware that the state-owned centre in Poznan, who feared competition from Warsaw, had previously been in touch with the local authorities in Warsaw to ensure that no planning permission would be granted to us. When Janus became aware of the dirty tricks, he quickly adjusted his game plan by submitting two sets of planning applications under different themes: the first an office block as a 'Polish Trade Centre'; the second an 'Expocentre'. Predictably, the Trade Centre application was approved and the Expocentre drawings were rejected. 'But Janus,' I protested, 'we do not have planning permission.' 'We have' came the reply. 'We have one for Trade Centre; now we build. They will not know until we finish that it is an Expocentre. Then we apply for occupancy; if we get it, all OK; if not, what will they do? The building is up; they will have to give permission.'

This kind of tenuous reasoning was the basis for more than 90 per cent of all real estate developments in Poland. In our case, the occupancy certificate was delayed for 12 months, but as Janus had predicted, consent was obtained in the end. We had succeeded, but at what price? The risk/reward ratio was our yardstick. In the period 2003 to 2006, as the risks diminished, so did the rewards. Value added tax (VAT) was introduced, together with a legal system that now provides clear title to land and each year the real estate market in Poland gets better; a far cry from the conditions when we entered.

There were also other problems in development projects. There were really no property surveyors in Poland as there are in other countries. We had to employ either our own engineers or qualified field workers from other countries to assist us in checking out the land prior to construction. In spite of all Janus's experience, we were faced with two dilemmas. First, when soil tests were being carried out we discovered a bomb shelter from World War II; and, second, the undersoil was wet due to flooding from an adjoining site owned, inevitably, by the government.

At that point, by a stroke of good luck or darker fate, Poland announced the privatization of its second-largest exhibition centre in Katowice. If we could secure ownership of the Katowice Centre, then with the Warsaw Expocentre we could become the largest venue operator in Poland. After months of negotiation we were short-listed and in the final stage of the selection process we won the tender for Katowice Centre, a 20,000 square-metre complex with 8 halls, of which one was recently constructed. Expomedia paid a total of US$5 million for a 51 per cent holding in the Katowice Centre company, with the remaining shares held by the Polish State Treasury.

In the course of tendering for the Katowice Centre we lost the opportunity to buy the Kielce Expocentre, which was also being privatized. It was bought by the Poznan Fair Corporation, a Polish venture owned by the State and a private investment partner. Our decision to invest in Katowice rather than Kielce was to come back to haunt us five years later.

With the Polish acquisitions behind us, we proceeded to go public on the AIM market of the London Stock Exchange. Thus, Expomedia Group Plc was born. Amro Ventures was overjoyed as it immediately placed its 40 per cent shareholding with other investors, realizing a substantial profit on its investment in less than 12 months. The shares were launched at 67 pence, with the company valued at £20 million or €30 million. Within six months of flotation, the Expomedia share price rose to £1.

The Expomedia Formula for rapid expansion was to partner with leading Media Groups having magazine and newspaper interests through joint ventures offering them the opportunity to 'go live', with exhibitions themed and backed by their own specialized publications and then promoted in their own newspapers to generate visitors. To that extent, Expomedia was successful in forging partnerships with some of the world's leading media and conference groups – The Telegraph Group, Daily Mail Group, Bertlesmann, Gazprom Media, Times of India, Informa and others. This partnership strategy was supplemented by the selective acquisition of trade fairs that we believed could prosper with the joint venture backing of the media groups. Brands would then be established and, in a matter of five to ten years, Expomedia could become the leading company in its field. Joint venturing gave the Group access to capital for acquisitions, which in many cases were funded by the media group for the benefit of the joint venture. Expomedia became the first company of its kind to succeed along these lines.

The Achilles heel to Expomedia's business plans were the
venues, which were intended to give the Group security of tenure
but also required heavy funding during the first three years, in
turn affecting the profit and loss account of the Expomedia
Company adversely. The media groups' supported the company
but wanted quicker results from the necessary infrastructure
investments in the emerging markets. In the early years, Expomedia operated at heavy losses, which impacted the Group's balance
sheet. While the company's assets and sales grew, so did the losses
and financial commitment on the venues. 'When will you be profitable?' I was asked repeatedly. 'This year I hope,' was my consistent reply. After four years, Expomedia was at last able to break
even and was positioned for further growth and profit in 2006.

To continue its expansion and reassure the City, Expomedia
decided to stop developing new shows and centres and launched
a licensing division. Through this, it would license any approved
company wishing to acquire exclusive rights to use Expomedia
know-how in new territories and countries where Expomedia did
not have any operations. In this way, the company could now go
forward concentrating on its core markets of India, Russia, Poland
and Germany. The licensing division would earn royalties on the
revenues generated in new markets once the licensees were established and Expomedia Group maintained the right to buy out any
licence, once profitable, on an exit formula. In short, Expomedia
Group would now generate profit from its core business, expand
in new territories without taking any risks and have the right to
consolidate by acquiring licences once profitable.

The licensing division reinvigorated Expomedia Group with
entrepreneurial spirit and grew parallel to it, completing the chain
of worldwide operations without investment and management
risks by the mother company.

At my 65th birthday in March 2005, I was nearing the end of
my fourth year at Expomedia. I confirmed my decision to step
down as Executive Chairman and continue as a non-executive
Director. Mark's reaction was somewhat sullen. 'Why now?' he

asked. 'In the next five years the company will be five to ten times its present size.' However, Mark appreciated my motives for leaving my 20 per cent shareholding in Expomedia to appreciate as he envisioned.

After four years, in January 2006, Expomedia Group was valued at €114 million or approximately four times its original investment value. Annual sales turnover was approaching €35 million with €5 million pre-tax profits projected for 2007. The Group had six exhibition centres and 30 established business operations with New Delhi, Warsaw, Katowice, Cologne, Belgrade, Amsterdam and Moscow venues in varying stages of planning and development. Expomedia Group was also the organizer of some 200 conferences and published 12 magazines.

On 27 January 2006, Mark addressed over 300 delegates at the third Annual Expomedia partners meeting in Marbella. The results for the past year could hardly have been better and were warmly applauded. In an upbeat message, he announced plans for 2006/2007, including joint ventures with a leading European Media Group with further joint ventures to follow. The partners left after the meeting and all the senior Expomedia directors stayed on for an extra two days to celebrate and rest.

Seated in the hotel lobby, Mark and I relaxed. 'Thank God they've all left.' I declared to the team. 'Sit down with us; you all did a great job.' I had arranged a birthday cake for Mark to celebrate his 36th birthday, which was served as we sat there. As Mark was cutting the cake, a secretary came running. 'Mark, Roger, there has been an accident. Can you step aside? I need to talk to you both. There is a problem in Poland at the Katowice Centre.' 'Tell them to deal with it; why have you disturbed us?' was my first reaction, not comprehending the nature or scale of the disaster. 'No, no. The roof has collapsed,' we were told. 'There are 60 people dead, 100 people missing and 30 per cent of the country has been declared a national disaster area. You are needed immediately.'

Needless to say, that was an unwanted birthday present for Mark. All his dreams and the efforts of his team were wiped out in a matter of hours, through no fault of our own. With no planes flying direct from Marbella to Poland, Warsaw Airport closed due to the heavy snow and all roads to Katowice blocked, we decided to charter a small plane and the whole management team left within six hours. We arrived early the next morning to view the wreckage and to see what could be done to help the victims and co-ordinate the helplines – a task that we had never envisaged for ourselves and for which we had neither training nor experience.

For Expomedia Group, the Katowice catastrophe was a major setback. Of course, there were insurance claims and possible lawsuits against the city architect and constructors who had built the Centre before it was privatised and prior to our investment. However, it seemed inevitable that our subsidiary would also be blamed for the authorities' shortcomings – a hard lesson to accept in one of the EU's recent new entrants.

For the next nine months the attention of our management was wholly focused on making sure that the insurance claims were processed, in disposing of the Group's interests in the Katowice Centre and ensuring that its main flagship centre in Warsaw continued to grow profitably in spite of the unfair adverse publicity. We disposed of our interests in the Katowice Centre to a Polish group who are better able to pursue the matter. Our reluctance to pursue the Polish authorities for selling us a defective centre has proved to be the correct strategy. Nevertheless, our experience illustrates the perils of engaging with governments of emerging market states, even in the case of the newer EU members.

Our competitors worldwide had a field day passing rumours about the financial stability of the group and contacting our clients with a view to converting them to their exhibition programmes. Our shareholders were supportive during this difficult period, and Mark and his team began the Herculean task of recovery and decided to sell and lease back all our centres. Never again would the company own its own centres.

The Group soon went back into profit in early 2007 on its path of fulfilling Mark's dream of turning the company over the next five years into a billion-dollar-plus leader in its field, and its battle-tested management were older and wiser.

After six months in my new role as Non-Executive Chairman, the Group decided to move to Watford. The new headquarters are more elegant and larger; and more importantly, the overhead cost is only one-third that of our former Chelsea office. Although I lived six blocks away in Chelsea, close by the old offices, it took me three hours' travel time for the round trip to the new office.

By contrast, Mark's journey time and that of other Expomedia Group Plc senior managers was greatly reduced and I wondered if they were conveying a not too subtle hint that it was time for me to take a back seat. In any case, for me the writing was already on the wall. At 66, I was beginning to feel bored once again and ready for new adventures.

This is the curse of the serial entrepreneur. As my friend Nicolas Berry accurately observes in his introduction, how to be an 'aprés-entrepreneur' is my problem. The truth is that creating opportunities and developing new businesses is my way of life. There are always tantalizing new ventures to consider and, for me, the conveyor belt never stops. Sometimes, I feel like a 21st century Flying Dutchman who was condemned to sail the seven seas for eternity without rest. However, there are always 'ships that pass in the night' and that is the consolation.

Chapter 12

How to Make it in Emerging Markets: As a Millionaire, Mega-millionaire or Oligarch Billionaire

Most of my business ventures with ITE and Expomedia have been in the emerging markets of Central and Eastern Europe and later in India, to which I can add my long experience of doing business in China. It is in these markets, with their higher rates of economic growth, 'flexible' approaches to regulation and ready acceptance of the entrepreneurial mindset that the greatest opportunities for aspiring paper millionaires arise today.

There is no magic formula for making millions in emerging markets, but they do have characteristics in common that distinguish them from Western markets and add to the perils, as well creating opportunity. Indeed, higher risk and greater opportunity are reverse sides of the emerging market coin. Nevertheless, there are simple, unwritten 'street-smart' guidelines, learnt only through personal experience on how to approach an emerging market for the first time, how to acquire knowledge of local codes of conduct and ever-changing business environments and how to establish a presence that apply in almost every case. In addition, there are other practical hints that are particular to each individual market.

The key message is that as an individual entrepreneur you need no capital of your own beyond the funding of your travel and living expenses for two years in order to graduate as a paper millionaire.

The first part of this chapter identifies the common features and behaviour tips that I have learned the hard way through experience.

The second part of the chapter consists of advice on how to develop your personal equity interest in your chosen venture, by reference to three case studies of successful projects. The first was mine and the two others are modelled on those of aspiring paper millionaires who observed the same general principles.

In the third part of the chapter I comment on the progression from paper millionaire to mega-millionaire and the perils of aspiring further to become an oligarch billionaire in Russia. As a postscript, my personal observations are included in the next and final chapter on the business environment for paper millionaires in each of the three global emerging markets of greatest opportunity.

COMMON APPROACHES

The first differentiator to apply by those seeking to gain entry to an emerging market is a clear definition of your objective. If you are looking for a big profit on a single trade deal, where you or your company have a leading edge product or technology, or a particular capacity to import from the target country, your strategy will be tailored accordingly. On the other hand, if you intend to engage in the local market in order to build a business of any kind over a longer period, your strategy and tactics will be quite different. Putting it crudely, are you looking for a 'one-night stand' or a long-term relationship of four to five years?

The second up-front decision to be made is to define for whom you are venturing forth:

- yourself (on your own)
- the company that employs you
- your government.

The advice I can offer hardly applies to government ventures, although there may be elements in the approach which I advocate that have some resonance with government representatives – if only as an explanation of why they frequently fail to achieve their objectives.

Whether you are a lone entrepreneur or an executive charged with a mission by your company to develop a longer-term business relationship, there is a further set of questions that you should ask yourself – and answer honestly:

Where do I start?

The selection of country and market that you seek to enter will probably be made for you by your company, if you are an employee, although you may be asked for some input in the decision-making process. Certainly, the product or service area will not be in question. As an entrepreneur on your own you have a much wider choice of both location and business scope.

You will probably make your primary choice of emerging market on the basis of published information and the anecdotal evidence of others you know who have set up in business there, but the choice of location within that market is a more subjective decision which you may prefer to make after you have visited and travelled about within the country. In my case, when entering the Russian market in the early 1990s, Moscow was the only sensible location because that is where my opportunities were offered. Today, as the Russian business environment has become more sophisticated and economic development is widespread, it makes better sense to focus instead on regional markets with populations over 1 million, such as Volgagrad, Nizny Novgorod, Yekaterinburg or Samara, where opportunities abound and regulation and planning consents are devolved to local authorities. Whether your chosen emerging market is the Czech Republic, Hungary, Poland, India or China, cities in the regions are now better starting points for aspiring paper millionaires than Prague, Budapest and Warsaw or, in the case of India or China, New Delhi, Beijing and Shanghai.

As to the choice of niche market in which to operate, the only limitation is the range of your skills and the activities in which you have had a successful experience. Wherever you go, acceptance by the local business community will depend upon the confidence that you generate as an expert in your field. In my case, I was able to secure the licences for exhibitions and to operate them successfully in Prague, Moscow, Kiev, Almaty and elsewhere because I had a track record in exhibition management. Therefore, if you have previous experience in, say, managing water treatment plants in the West, you are qualified and eligible to go for a licence to build a water treatment plant in a regional location. Don't attempt to involve yourself in office, supermarket or property developments unless you have credible real estate development experience. 'Follow your *métier*' is the golden rule.

How big a business do I want to build?

Be very clear in your own mind how big you want your venture to be, in terms of annual sales, cash flow or profits. More importantly, decide what your personal objectives are, in terms of the value you want to generate for your stake in the business when the time comes to exit, either by cashing in or floating your company. Your personal objectives will define the parameters of the business. As the second golden rule, your business model should start with the desired end result and work backwards to the start.

How long should it take to reach my goal?

This question requires little debate. Given the high-risk, fast-changing business environment of the emerging market into which you are about to plunge, you should set yourself a firm target of two years maximum in which to achieve your objective. In practice, you should target yourself to accomplish the business-building task within 18 months, allowing yourself six months to negotiate and make arrangements for the capitalization of your investment.

Personal commitment – am I free?

As an independent entrepreneur, you will need to devote the whole of your time for at least two years to your business venture, living mostly abroad at the location of your project. If you are a paid employee, your company must commit 100 per cent of your time to the project for the same period, while funding your relocation and living expenses.

Return visits to your home base need to be strictly rationed. For you to succeed, your local partners and associates need to have the perception that you are there for the duration. This is an absolute requirement and, on this point above all, you need to be honest with yourself. If you are unmarried and free from family obligations, the decision to leave home for two years is not too difficult. For the married with young children, living away from home for two years may not be an acceptable condition. If that is the case, you will need a reliable partner who is prepared to live locally with you.

Starting up without investment capital

Having chosen the location for your venture, you need to install yourself there in order to cultivate relationships and associations with local business operators and professionals in your selected field with whom you might do business. At the outset, you may not have a clear idea of the business activity in which you will engage and the personal relationships that you develop will be an important determinant in your final choice.

To that end you must be ready to integrate socially on equal terms with your prospective business partners – in the modern vernacular, 'to walk the walk and talk the talk.' This criterion helps you to define your lifestyle and the kind of accommodation that you should choose for yourself. A simple one-bedroom apartment is all that you will need as a single person and your budget can be tailored accordingly.

How much should you budget?

As an example, the monthly living cost without travel for a single person in Moscow in the mid-1990s for accommodation and food was US$3,000, and is about US$5,000 today in 2007. If you are taking your wife or a partner with you, increase your budget by 50 per cent and add on 10 per cent for travel. Therefore, today on your own you will need a budget of US$132,000 to cover your expenses over the 24-month period of your stay, excluding the cost of flights to and from home. In the regions of Russia you can get by on 40 per cent less or $80,000 for two years

Is it a positive or negative to go alone?

We come back to the question of whether or not you should take your wife or partner with you. Whatever the advantages of having your permanent companion by your side with whom you can share the experience and mull over the progress of your project, on balance you will find that the adage 'he travels fastest who travels alone' applies.

There are two reasons for my conclusion. First, with the possible exception of China, the business community that you are seeking to enter will be male-dominated socially and, unless she is a local national, your companion will have difficulty in being accepted or in making any contribution. Second, and more selfishly, if you have 'freedom to roam' there is much to be gained with the many intelligent and attractive women whom you may encounter. As you have read, the women in my story who became my companions all contributed greatly in helping me to accelerate my learning curve in understanding local culture, mindsets and attitudes to business. Some of them in positions of authority or influence made important interventions in the development of my business ventures. In all cases, their warm friendship and the time spent with them were vital ingredients in achieving my success and gaining fluency in the Russian language.

For these reasons, and in light of my experience of the disruptive effects on my personal life and family relationships, I have come to a second conclusion. Those with youth and sufficient experience but without family attachments aged, say, 28–30, or those over 55 with understanding wives and grown-up families are the most suited to the life of the entrepreneurial adventurer in emerging markets. After all, the absence of a partner for two years who will return with $25–50 million or more is unlikely to deter any *fiancée* or distress a mature partner. After 25 years of marriage most wives would give their husbands two years' leave of absence against an assurance that he can return with as much as $50 million. Many, I suspect, would say 'If it takes you three years, that'll be fine. Let me help you pack your bags'.

DEVELOPING THE VENTURE AND YOUR EQUITY INTEREST

Whatever kind of business you wish to develop, the basic strategy and tactics are much the same. Once installed in your chosen location, you will need to carry out fact-finding to discover how your business sector is organized, its structure, the legal framework within which it operates, how authorizations and licences to operate are granted, who are the key players, what are the opportunities for you and who are the facilitators who can best help you to make contacts and establish relationships. An early priority is to form a friendly business association with someone who can help you to procure an extended multi-entry visa to replace the single-entry visa originally issued to you. Having identified the people with whom you hope to do business, you will set out to make their acquaintance by tapping into their social network. This exercise will involve much socializing in restaurants, hotels and clubs, through which you will establish your presence there on a permanent basis as a knowledgeable, competent business-man with limited personal means, but with access to capital in your home market, who can be trusted. There are no shortcuts in this groundwork to establish yourself as an acceptable business associate.

'Small is beautiful – and safe'

Next, a word about the scale of operations. When deciding how big you want your venture to be in terms of sales, cash flow or profits, it is advisable to shoot for an ultimate valuation of US$25 million up to a maximum of US$50 million. In today's emerging markets, when your project fills a void, it is not difficult to gener-ate profits of US$3–5 million within three to four years. This will enable any start-up to list on a stock exchange in Europe – such as the AIM market in London – with a valuation of US$20–50 million and upwards.

Investment brokers' criteria

For an emerging market, serious investors or stockbrokers base their decisions on the following criteria:

- whether your company's product or service really fills a void in that market
- the quality and previous track record of the management
- whether the company stands a good chance of becoming the market leader.

To go public and list your shares on the AIM market of the London Stock Exchange, the technical requirement of three years' operation for a listing can be readily overcome. This can be done through the acquisition of an established local company with at least a three-year record that could be funded as part of the placement of shares, if the need arises

In most cases that I have known, entrepreneurs who started small were able to move on to bigger and more profitable ventures, having established their first small success in these emerging markets. For an aspiring millionaire, doing bigger deals is more difficult at the outset. Starting small offers you a better chance of success.

CASE STUDY 'A': PROPERTY DEVELOPMENT
The funding principles and development approach that I use here in a regional centre of Russia can apply equally to hotel, supermarket and office or apartment block projects. This is not only the case in Russia's regions but in any of the CIS Republics' or in the regions of countries further afield, which have only partially abandoned command economy practices.

The mantra of 'location, location, location' applies in emerging markets as in any part of the world, but a critical factor which cannot be ignored, and may take precedence, is your ability to secure access to land at virtually no cost or at the original cost to the person or company that owns the land in question. Having lined up the alternative locations where the land is available on this basis, you then narrow down the shortlist to those locations that you believe would be best for your project.

In Russia, particularly in the regions outside Moscow, many companies, plants and local administrations own or have access to land for development, but may not know how to go about a development project, let alone understand the principles of how to attract foreign investment capital and for which project.

In one regional centre where I focused my attention I was interested in building a hotel plus an accompanying business centre together with an apartment complex, for which the land requirement was 2.5 hectares. My first calls when I visited this 1-million-plus population city were to the local Chamber of Commerce and a group of local real estate agents, asking them if they could identify companies and entities that owned or had access to suitable plots of land for my project. I told them that it was my intention to establish a group that would ultimately invest US$25 million on the project if the necessary site could be obtained at nominal or nil cost.

On several further visits, I was offered various sites for sale at the full commercial price. I shared my frustrations with the local realtors and city officials, explaining that while I had access to the money to fund the construction, the land had to be acquired at cost meaning 'virtually free', to entice investors to invest in this region. I also asked for introductions to some plot owners and offered each of them a joint venture (JV), in which they would put their land in as paid-up capital at US$5 million (present commercial value). This would be in return for a 20 per cent share of the project weere we to invest the US$25 million required for the development. My plan at the time was a three-step approach as follows

Phase 1 – a hotel of 120 rooms
Phase II – a business centre (an office block of 8–10,000 square metres)
Phase III – an apartment block (100 apartments) of 6,000 square metres.

This strategy would offer a safe way for all participants to proceed one step at a time with the appropriate proportion of land to be released for each succeeding phase.

Without planning permission and construction permits to build all three phases the JV would, of course, be worthless. Therefore, I proposed that the plot owners, with their local connections, should take responsibility for this critical task while we would contribute the cost of the topographical study of the plot and the design fees for detailed architectural drawings. Normally in the regions of Russia, the final design/architectural costs barely exceed US$250,000–300,000 for such projects.

The several owners considered my proposal in the knowledge that our project was the only one on offer, and on the understanding that we would conclude a deal with whoever accepted our offer first.

At the same time, I was working on how to raise the US$300,000 required for the detailed design/architectural costs and what security I could ask for and offer to investors at this very early stage. In the meantime, I approached the local Chamber of Commerce again to ask if it could be a partner. As a quasi-government agency, the Chamber could requisition land for its development from the local authority if we could offer to finance the project. We reached a preliminary agreement that in exchange for a 2.5-hectare site we would pay a tax to the local government for a 'lease in perpetuity' (99 years or more) – in other words for an indefinite term – with an annual ground rent of approximately US$5,000. After one year, we could apply to the local government to purchase the freehold of the constructed buildings at a very low nominal price. In consideration of the transfer of its rights to the 2.5-hectare plot, the Chamber requested us to build for them a small office block of approximately 500 square metres. In the context of the overall 30,000 square metres that we intended to construct, the cost of the Chamber's land participation was less than US$400,000 (or less than 5 per cent) as a proportion of the US$25 million to be invested.

The outcome of our open offer to other plot owners was that we received five acceptances. We proceeded to select the best location from the five. All of this took place over a period of six months, during which we befriended all the local authorities and principals. We took care to be frank, ensuring that they knew not only that we were working as a team with the various other plot owners and local chambers on the same basis but that the Western banks would make the final project selection based on their advisers' recommendation, not ours.

I prepared a JV contract in the name of a new company that I formed as sole shareholder. The company required US$25 million to carry out the development that would yield a minimum of US$50 million once sold outright on completion. Alternatively, I calculated that if the US$25 million were borrowed in the UK, the entire amount could be repaid in four to five years, thereafter yielding 25 per cent per annum, an almost unheard of rate of return on investment (ROI) in the West. Of course, the greater the return, the greater the risk during the building process. Hence the adage 'keep your projects small.' In our case, Phase I required US$7 million; Phase II would be undertaken only after completion of the first phase. Naturally, once construction was complete, the entire plot would be re-valued for loan purposes to finance the next stage.

I made two trips to London to meet with colleagues of mine in the property field and gave several of them options to get in on the ground floor as partners, in return for providing the US$300,000 (approximately £150,000) required to secure planning consent for the project. Several of the parties who I contacted were property funds that had previously purchased and financed projects in Russia, providing a yield of 14 per cent. As a result of the competition from other funds, they were now facing higher prices for finished buildings, offering reduced yields of 11–12 per cent, in spite of the risk factors for Russia.

I also contacted various hotel management companies, procuring offers to manage the hotel and, at the same time, their design recommendations for the hotel part of the development. Foreign builders had been invited to quote for the development and their firm offers would be forthcoming, once the final architectural design had been approved.

Within 12 months, the level of interest was sufficiently high for us to take the decision to build the first complex and also to add a second project. This involved a shopping centre of approximately

20,000 square metres, at a cost of US$15 million, which would also pay for itself over four years and yield a 25 per cent return.

On the other side, the Russian partners were elated by all the blue-chip names of institutions, builders and others that we were bringing to their region. They began to offer more projects to us, such as a 'cinemaplex', aquaparks and fitness centres, all of which we declined, saying that we were fully occupied with what we had on hand to ensure that all went well.

In summary, after giving up equity 'kickers' to procure the US$25 million necessary for the project and looking after the Russian partners' interests, we ended up with a 52 per cent equity position in the development, that was projected to yield at least US$5 million annually. Alternatively, if we exited both projects, having packaged them over 18 months including the period of obtaining planning permission, we could expect to realize US$22 million after paying everybody off.

This venture really was 'what dreams are made of'. However, 18 months spent in a remote region where the temperature was 30 degrees below zero the previous winter is a stiff price to pay; but then, if you are self-starter you can't afford to be a cheeky beggar. Why not emulate Clint Eastwood, who endured the making of a couple of spaghetti westerns and returned as a world class movie star, maybe saving the 5–6 years that it would have taken him to be 'discovered' by Hollywood. I am sure that he had more fun with Italians enacting Red Indians and whatever else it took for his early movies to achieve 'classic status'.

CASE STUDY 'B' – INDUSTRIAL PLANTS OR MACHINERY

With the present dependence of the Russian economy on the energy sector, the industrial sector, save for oil- and gas-related equipment, is largely neglected. More than 100,000 Russian factories are either in disrepair or idle and unlimited opportunities exist today for re-tooling small factories to manufacture products that Russia needs badly and currently imports. Many Russian companies have good basic facilities, with spare production capacity and excellent sales and distribution networks, not only within Russia but also throughout the CIS. Whether in frozen food, confectionery, medical products or furniture, you name it, wherever there is a void, there is the opportunity for entrepreneurs to fill it and make a small fortune in the next 3 years, from 2007 through to 2010 with less than 1,000 days left.

Under this scenario, after carrying out the necessary research by visits to several relevant trade fairs covering the products that you intend to launch, you will be able to access the companies direct and see for yourself whether there are opportunities before planning your next step. If you are convinced that what you have in mind is needed or is far superior to that which is available in the Russian market, take a deep breath and go for it.

Meet with those companies that you have selected, telling them that you wish to co-manufacture such a product in Russia and ask whether there is spare capacity in their factories. The terms of your proposal are that, if they will provide the manufacturing facility, you will provide the tooling or necessary machinery with the finished product to be distributed through their distribution channels. Quality assurance that would be enhanced and maintained to ensure the final quality and pricing would be under your control.

A JV could be created in the form of a new company that would import and pay for the necessary machinery and equipment to manufacture the proposed product. The company could sign an outsourcing manufacturing contract for the use of the Russian company's facilities, with an option to transfer the entire manufacturing process to a new plant at some time in the future.

During your negotiations with the various companies, you will learn a great deal as you befriend your new colleagues who might have better ideas than those with which you started. Most Russian companies were frustrated for many years as their products lagged behind those of Western manufacturers – the latter enjoying marketing and design budgets and investments in quality assurance. Their frustration has spurred many of them on to launch new products today with less investment but better packaging.

As an example, in less than three years, a Russian fruit juice provider was transformed into the market leader, while competing with Tropicana and other imported brands. So successful was he that he was able to go public on the London Stock Exchange with the help of two entrepreneurs who provided the funds for new packaging machinery and marketing. Almost overnight he became a US$600-million company, which rejected many takeover offers from leading foreign juice manufacturers.

If the company to whom you are talking is open to a takeover in the form of an injection of share capital, a deal could evolve whereby they provide their present facilities and real estate at zero cost on their books and you provide the capital for packaging and other machinery in exchange for a 50 per cent shareholding for each party.

In many cases, well-known brands that you are trying to emulate may agree to advance the sums required for machinery, training and quality assurance systems. By way of illustration, if US$1–3 million are required for your project, you might be able to entice a European manufacturer to provide funding with an option to purchase an equity stake in the company. This would give them a formula for the eventual buy-out of your shares at a pre-agreed multiple or price. Sooner or later, this household product brand leader, manufacturing abroad, will be seeking entry to the Russian market.

Again, your prior credentials in the field will play an important part. Having worked in the trade yourself or put together the experienced management team to supervise the project, you will have the necessary credentials to give comfort to the European company that they will be dealing with professionals in their own field. Alternatively, a business plan could be drawn up for investors to finance the small amount of start-up capital required, with the prospect of a listing on the AIM market in one or two years, which would enable them to exit with a reward of 10 times their original investment. On the other hand, an even greater pay-out exit could be achieved if the JV company is taken over by a major foreign manufacturer wishing to use it as a base for the introduction of other products into Russia.

Whatever the structure, the opportunity to put together a floatable company structure with little or no capital outlay required on the part of the entrepreneur exists only in the emerging markets where he has undertaken the preliminary groundwork. In the process, he will have laid the foundation for an established company to take over a ready-made structure, which will accelerate its entry into these markets.

CASE STUDY 'C' – BOTTLED WATER

In Russia's two biggest cities, there currently exists just two home bottling plants producing bottled water from local springs, in competition with more than 50 brands of imported water from Vittel, Perrier, Evian and others. Therefore, if you choose to start a water-bottling facility and are free to explore and travel, go to the regions and investigate where all the springs are located. You will find hundreds of natural springs in every corner of every region in Russia.

Having narrowed down your search to say five, of the 30 regions with populations over 1 million, you have an excellent chance of launching a company with a potential capitalization of US$50 million or more if complementary products are added.

Your first step in tapping the local spring water resources is to make an offer to the local councils that control the springs within their areas, which they will accept. Almost 95 per cent of all springs in Russia are left to nature, unattended, with Russian motorists stopping by to fill huge containers for their weekly use and consumption at weekends. For example, next to my dacha on the outskirts of Moscow, my chauffeur stops by, almost as a ritual, to fill two two-gallon plastic containers from our local spring, one for our home and one for his family.

In any region, a local council would be only too pleased to sign over a 50-year renewable lease of the springs and adjoining land for a small bottling plant to be established locally. For the council, the benefits are employment and training for 20-50 locals and taxes on the production that it would use to maintain an area that at present is laid to pasture.

The second step is to check rigorously the quality of the water. Since all the local residents drink from the spring (and are still alive), checks must have been made previously by the water authority. A copy of the report should be available free and for an investment of US$200 a quick translation into English can be made.

The third step is to check the cost of preparing a small bottling facility and the equipment that would be required. Second-hand bottling equipment is readily available on the market for a modest investment of about US$200,000. New equipment on lease would also not represent a major investment. With the land and raw materials free of charge and plastic bottles available from any of the two dozen recently launched plastic bottle manufacturing plants, you will be ready to give your venture the green light.

A company would be formed that would enter into a JV with one, two or up to five regions owned by the entrepreneur. Provision of the necessary capital, whether US$250,000 (if the equipment were to be leased) or US$3 million for launching three–five individual brands would be offered to prospective investors. It would also possibly be offered to Russian companies presently distributing the major foreign-imported and branded waters in Moscow, St Petersburg and the regions. Local residents in the regions will always prefer to continue drinking their local brands and, of course, enjoying the price advantage.

Once established, these small regional water-bottling units could readily be sold on to their larger counterparts as the market consolidates, thereby providing exits for the investors and the entrepreneur.

This third case study is based on the actual initiative of the local marketing manger of a major brand distributor in Moscow who resigned from his company. He saw the future potential of handling regional water bottling plants on behalf of his foreign parent company, which invested US$4 million in his two-year pilot operation to prepare the complete package. He now has a seat on the board of the Russian distribution company and plans an Independent Public Offering (IPO), which will value his company at US$60 million. The IPO will offer 20 per cent of the shares for US$8 million to repay debt and provide additional capital for expansion. His exit is assured via a sale of 50 per cent of his holding to his previous employer, a pre-condition of its original financial support of his company.

Both the entrepreneur and his former employer benefited from this arrangement. If he had remained an employee, he would be making a low six-figure salary, whereas he now has a directorship and an 80 per cent equity stake in his own company, valued post-IPO at US$60 million plus. His former employer will acquire up to 50 per cent of the entrepreneur's equity stake for US$30 million in the five regional plants. Thus, the company's future expansion over other main competition brands is assured and the entrepreneur retains more than 40 per cent of the equity in the company.

The limiting factor

Your project will stand or fall on your ability to fund the development through Western banks and/or to procure Western investors, who will buy shares in your company either before or on a stock market flotation. In our example, the covenant of an established international hotel group as the operator of the hotel would be a prerequisite to raising bank loans for the development. Equally, you need to be sure of identifying equity investors with a taste for hotels, supermarkets, offices and apartment complexes, in order to establish a market value for your equity.

I have already highlighted the importance of your personal credibility and experience at the outset in the relevant field of activity in order to attract local partners. These personal credentials will also be required subsequently to gain the confidence and support of investors or the stock exchange on which your company's shares are to be floated and of the brokers and other professionals who are essential to the process.

For those with funds

If you are assigned to an emerging market project by your employer, you may expect a greater degree of comfort in your accommodation and daily living. If you are already on your own but have deeper pockets, you can also decide to live more comfortably but the same two-year time commitment with semi-permanent residence is required. However, living in a 4- or 5-star hotel would have the disadvantage of suggesting that you are affluent and make it more difficult to develop local relationships on equal terms.

On the other hand, as an employee, you would have the advantage of going for the first time, perhaps to attend a trade fair, at your company's expense and of measuring at the same time the level of interest and opportunity for a project of your own. If your findings are positive and you have the courage to abandon your security and strike out on your own, go home and resign, then return as an entrepreneur.

MEGA MILLIONAIRE OR OLIGARCH BILLIONAIRE

So far I have focused on single-project development but, in the case of emerging market business ventures, one thing certainly leads to another. Your first successful project should be the hardest and will open up further opportunities as your business reputation and circle of local associates expands. Provided that you can continue to rely on your local partners and influential contacts to handle the issues involving authorizations, licences and registrations, there is only one barrier to repeating and multiplying your successes. At some point, your activities are likely to attract the attention of local groups of 'born again' capitalists or racketeers tolerated by the local government who will demand a share or control of your business. If you can avoid or overcome that obstacle, the path from millionaire to mega-millionaire or billionaire is clear.

In the case of ITE, we were able to deflect the interest of the 'local groups' in Moscow for a time because most of our revenues were collected in advance from Western exhibitors outside Russia through a UK-registered company paying UK taxes whose affairs were completely transparent. There was no scope for siphoning off hard currency income at source and the local currency revenues from Russian exhibitors and exhibition visitors were not enough to be attractive. However, as the scope of ITE's activities was extended further, I realized that we could not hope to continue 'flying below the radar' of the local groups' attention. This prompted our decision to transfer the management of local exhibitions to our Russian partners and, ultimately, to go public to sell our ITE shareholdings.

If you want to progress from millionaire to mega-millionaire or billionaire status in any emerging market, you will almost certainly have to accommodate local partners with the influence to handle 'business environment barriers' and exclusive concessions, introducing elements of unquantifiable commercial and even personal risk. As risk-takers rather than gamblers, Roddy and I did not consider that level of risk to be acceptable.

The ultimate progression from mega-millionaire to oligarch status demands an even greater exposure to risk and cannot be achieved without government involvement, giving access to privileged and exclusive playing fields by accommodating the financial interests of highly placed government associates. Fishing in these deep waters carries high risks both to your wealth and your personal safety. Unpredictable changes in political regimes, government power structures or the fortunes of your local partners, or any involvement in politics can result in your business being taken away from you, as Mikhail Khordokovsy of Yukos fame discovered to his cost. In his case, the stripping of most of his wealth was accompanied by a long-term prison sentence.

Others have been less or more fortunate. With the financial success of *Forbes* magazine in covering Russian business, its Moscow Editor, Paul Klebnikov, decided to push the boundaries of Russian journalism. Following the successful publication of his detailed chronicle of the rise of the oligarchs on gangster capitalism (*Godfather of the Kremlin, 2000, Harcourt Inc., US*) he was shot down by 'an unknown assailant'.

On a personal note, my Russian colleague and friend over the last 14 years, Edouard was shot through the back of the head by a professional hitman, as disclosed by the police. Having built up a small fortune over the years working for ITE, Edouard decided to expand into the fast lane world of oil and gas. Perhaps these new activities led to his demise. Another theory is that he befriended the ex-wife of one of Russia's rising oligarchs, thereby mixing power with politics. Since leaving ITE in 1999, I had kept in touch with Eddy in his new *milieu,* where only the ruthless or the lucky survive.

Billionaire Marc Rich, a former US whiz kid oil trader who made his original fortune in the 1970s before fleeing to Switzerland in 1983 after indictment under the RICOH Act and for illegal oil trading with Iran (as reported on 2001 Cable News Network), re-emerged in 1990. With an Interpol 'red notice' on his head prioritizing his apprehension, he remained on the run until pardoned by US President Clinton.

In contrast, Boris Berezovsky, the most outrageous of the oligarchs and the main character in *Godfather of the Kremlin,* who was alleged in the book to have pillaged the commanding heights of the Russian economy by exploiting his political influence throughout the period of the Yeltsin presidency, is wanted in Russia to this day for criminal misdealing. Although he has asylum in the UK and lives quietly in London, innocent or not, he can hardly have peace of mind so long as the Russian claim for his extradition remains outstanding.

Chapter 13

The Key Emerging Markets

Of course, there are business opportunities for aspiring paper millionaires in carefully selected niches of all emerging markets. However, there are more exceptional opportunities in the three key country markets of Russia, China and India than in other countries, by reason of their size, both geographically and in terms of population, their exceptionally high GDP growth and the potential of their consumer demand. As the postscript to this book, the reflections that follow are my personal commentary on each very different business environment.

RUSSIA

There is still the 'space' to become a paper millionaire or billionaire in Russia. Even during the periods of gross economic mismanagement under Mikhail Gorbachev and Boris Yeltsin, as successive Russian governments attempted to transform a command economy to an open market economy, it was always possible for both local and foreign private entrepreneurs to make money. The value of personal savings was decimated by hyperinflation at the end of the 1980s and the remaining wealth of Russian citizens was destroyed by the banking crisis and virtual bankruptcy of the State in 1998. Corruption, always endemic in Russia, escalated in the early 1990s, when 'gangsterism' became rife, culminating in the Great Mob War of 1993–1994. In the second half of the 1990s, the pillars of Russian industry were privatized and in some cases, manipulated voucher and auction schemes were devised and carefully orchestrated by the government and its cronies, placing controlling shareholdings in the hands of a small, self-selected band of oligarchs. In contrast to the privileged few gangster capitalists who were beneficiaries of the near-destruction of the economy, most Russian people received no benefit. The history of this whole period of misrule is recorded in amazingly well documented detail in Paul Klebnikov's book, *'Godfather of the Kremlin'*.

And yet, during this period, I was able to start up and grow the ITE exhibition business in Russia and the CIS with minimal interference from these disruptive elements that crippled the ventures of many other Western entrepreneurs. How was this accomplished? Undoubtedly, I was fortunate in my choice of Russian partners who served me well and benefited handsomely from the businesses they developed, for themselves through ITE and from the final cash-out of their ITE shares. I was also careful to keep a low profile personally, happy for my Russian associates to take the limelight and become well known in Moscow as exhibition management entrepreneurs. I was careful to steer clear of any possible business association with those who were involved in government politics. Finally, as already mentioned, I was sensitive to the appropriate time for exit.

My approach to building a business as an entrepreneur in Russia is fully explained in the previous chapter in the examples that I have cited.

CHINA

The business environment

China is the largest emerging market and the first after the 'Asian Tigers' of Singapore, South Korea, Taiwan and Thailand to take the trail towards a modern industrial economy. Under the dictatorship of Chairman Mao and the 'Gang of Four' that succeeded him, China showed little sign of becoming internationally competitive, let alone the achievements to come of the past 25 years. Principally an agrarian economy, the Chinese leaders focused their industrial efforts on defence and heavy industry, importing their largely outdated technology from Russia. However, Chinese ingenuity, skills and a limitless labour force propelled China into becoming a conventional military and nuclear power.

Then, in 1979, everything changed when the new paramount leader Deng Xaioping announced his 'open door' policy while touring southern China. The cornerstone of the country's economic renaissance was the Joint Venture Law which was introduced that year and which, for the first time, brought a degree of commercial certainty for foreign investors entering China. Written in relatively unambiguous English, the Joint Venture Law was open to varying interpretations by the Ministries and local approval authorities and was hardly a satisfactory basis for legal dispute or Western lawyers to work with. Surprisingly, there were no major amendments to the Joint Venture Law until 1990 and the national Chinese Company Law was not introduced until 1993, several years after my trade exhibition activities in China came to an end.

Until quite recently, there was little point in using Western lawyers for commercial transactions in China except as a comfort blanket for company executives who could tell their shareholders that they had taken the 'best advice available'. Even today, now that there is a complex body of commercial law and regulations, ambiguity abounds and it is difficult to pretend that the rule of law prevails. A major cause of uncertainty is the interpretation that provincial and municipal governments may differ from a relatively clear central government interpretation in Beijing. Indeed, many of the small-print regulations are not available in foreign language translation, including English. Therefore, while the big international law firms are now raking in fees through their Beijing and Shanghai offices, my first advice to entrepreneurs is to seriously consider 'going it alone'. Rely instead on agreements in clear business language for which Chinese partners are able to gain the authorities' approval.

If you find yourself in dispute with your Chinese partners after the deal is done and you cannot resolve your differences through 'friendly discussions' – the Chinese euphemism for tough negotiation – the best conclusion may be to walk away and write off your investment in time and money.

Remember too that the Chinese perception of legal contracts is quite different from that of most Western business people and their advisers.

For the Chinese, no contract is fixed in stone; it is no more than a snapshot of what the parties agreed at the time. As the relationship and the venture develop, the Chinese expect the contract to evolve and alter.

The paper millionaire's approach is much the same, but this may be a problem for corporates, particularly American companies that remain among the most litigious on earth.

The political context

Don't be too put off that China remains a communist country with few pretensions of democracy. Only a tiny proportion of China's 1.3 billion population are members of the Chinese Communist Party; membership is by invitation only although not often refused. Without communism as a tool of organization, it is unlikely that the unification of China and its evolution into modern China could have occurred. The past excesses of Chairman Mao's regime are long gone and the emphasis of the government and all Chinese people is on continuing growth of the economy and a rising standard of living.

There is an unwritten social compact between educated Chinese and the government: so long as the government continues to deliver steady improvement in their income and wealth, the people will accept the constraints on their political and social behaviour and censorship of the media in domestic affairs. Thanks to the advent of international television channels, delivered by satellite and the Internet, censorship of external news and entertainment has dwindled. The government and most Chinese citizens are agreed that their priority is to get the economy right and establish China's economic world leadership before worrying too much about the political system. Their worst case scenario is the disorder and disastrous economy of Russia in the post-Soviet and pre-Putin era.

Then and now

The entrepreneurial instinct runs deep in most Chinese. That has always been evident in the Chinese diaspora throughout Asia and in the immigrant Chinese communities of America and Britain. The creation of wealth through family businesses is entirely consistent with the Confucian ethics on which Chinese society is still firmly based after nearly 60 years of communist government. And so, it is no surprise that entrepreneurial activity soon blossomed among state and city-owned enterprises after 1979. When I first visited China in the early 1980s, there was little sign of the rapid growth in the co-operatives or the emergence of private businesses that was to follow. However, governments of the municipalities and cities in the forefront of the new China had already adopted internationalist strategies to attract foreign investment and trade. My first exhibitions were staged in Tianjin, where the municipal government was particularly enlightened, and which served as the meeting point for adventurous Western businesses with a wide variety of the local government-owned businesses. Some bizarre negotiations ensued, of which the following encounter provides a vignette.

★

CASE STUDY – GET THE PICTURE

In June 1985, we organized an international trade exhibition in Tianjin in partnership with CCPIT Tianjin at which a wide variety of equipment manufacturers from Europe exhibited their products. Among those was the then British market leader in coin-operated photography kiosks, Photo-Me International Ltd, whose objective was to sell a large number of their kiosks for installation in Chinese cities, starting in Tianjin. Through my company ICE, we found a Tianjin Government-owned enterprise – a wholesale distributor of supplies to the city's major department stores who believed that local citizens would be attracted to buying passport-sized photographs of themselves and their families. There were no meeting rooms at the exhibition hall and so we arranged to meet in my bedroom after dinner one evening at the Tianjin Palace Hotel, a vast dark grey concrete building with a neo-classical entrance, constructed to a barracks-like Russian design. The furnishings of the cavernous interior was no improvement on the forbidding exterior.

The meeting was attended by the general manager, his deputy, another assistant and an interpreter. On the Western side, there was the managing mirector of Photo-Me International and the company's agent from Hong Kong, who acted as his interpreter but also insisted on adding his opinions to the debate. He wore a large gold Rolex bracelet watch, spoke loudly and created an immediately unfavourable impression on the Chinese. My role in the ensuing discussion was more that of a referee in a boxing match than an unbiased intermediary.

It was soon apparent that there was a real difficulty in concluding a transaction. Photo-Me International wanted to sell 20 kiosks for cash but were prepared to accept irrevocable letters of credit. The Chinese company had no cash and wanted a barter trade with product from stock. As an opening shot, the Chinese offered 20,000 sets in porcelain of 'The Emperor's Horses', a well-known artefact in the West but hardly in great demand. This offer was declined politely but treated with scorn by the Hong Kong agent.

As an alternative, the Chinese general manager offered 300,000 pairs of men's corduroy trousers. There was no real price discussion because no one could say what the value of the Chinese product was. By now, the Hong Kong agent was so distressed that he was jumping up and down on my bed screaming. Plainly, there was no meeting of minds and no deal was struck that evening.

As our relationship with Tianjin Municipal People's Government blossomed, we were offered, as trusted partners, an increasing flow of business opportunities, mainly in the form of joint venture projects. These opportunities to participate in Tianjin's ambitious growth plans ranged from JVs in mechanical engineering to business services, including the construction of an exhibition centre locally. The ultimate project, originally my brainchild but taken up enthusiastically by Tianjin, was the development of a China Trade Centre in London's Docklands.

The progress of the Docklands project referred to in the case study that follows is just one example of how imaginative investment opportunities with Chinese partners can be thrown away by a lack of corresponding imagination and greed on the part of Western developers and investors matched by government indifference.

CASE STUDY – CHINESE TAKEAWAY

Starting in 1984 and through the two years following I was able to gain the approval in principle of the London Docklands Development Corporation (LDDC) to the development of a China Trade Centre and Cultural City at the then undeveloped Canary Wharf in the Docklands. My company – ICE Group – in alliance with a consortium of investors and property developers, and in partnership with Tianjin Municipal People's Government, undertook to provide the funding and carry out the development to plans commissioned by ICE. In order to assist in gaining Chinese Central Government approval, I persuaded Lord Wilson – the former British Prime Minister and a strong supporter of China – to join the Board of ICE. He played an important role in winning the approval of the government for the project and in obtaining Tianjin's participation. ICE and the consortium secured an option to purchase land from the LDDC on favourable terms and the project seemed set fair for fruition.

For the purposes of illustrating my theme of lost opportunity, only a summary of the debacle that followed is necessary. The consortium that forced my withdrawal from ICE failed to exercise the option to buy into the planned China Trade Centre and ICE was unable to deliver under its agreement with Tianjin. The Tianjin negotiating team, headed by a former senior Bank of China officer, had acted throughout with complete sincerity and were sympathetic but understandably decided to negotiate direct with the LDDC. With characteristic patience, the delegation continued discussions for more than a year but reluctantly abandoned their mission when the real estate developer, which had replaced ICE as its partner, and the LDDC tripled the price of the land from the terms that I had negotiated originally. The Tianjin Government were defeated only by the greed and conflicting agendas of UK property developers and LDDC board members who had jockeyed for position throughout the life of the project.

At no time throughout the saga did the UK Government show any interest in the project. With that marvellous gift of 20/20 hindsight vision with which all unfulfilled entrepreneurs are afflicted, it is now clear that a great opportunity was missed, not just by ICE and its shareholders but by the LDDC and the British economy, to assume a pole position in the development of then emerging Sino-European trade.

I now realize now that there is a parallel between the fate of the Docklands China Trade Centre and the handover of Hong Kong to the People's Republic of China by Margaret Thatcher's Conservative Government.

In the late 1980s, when I was a frequent visitor to China, there was a surprisingly low-key interest in the discussions with Britain on the future of Hong Kong. Of more interest to our Chinese friends was the confrontation between Margaret Thatcher and Deng Xiao Ping on her only visit to Beijing, when she famously stumbled on her ascent of the steps to the Great Hall of the People where the meeting was held. The antipathy between the two was obvious to everyone. Lady Thatcher is said to have commented that Mr Deng was the coldest and most ruthless man she had ever met and he is reported to have said much the same about her. The Chinese judged that they were evenly matched in terms of iron resolve and expected that protracted negotiations would ensue over a period of years.

Therefore, the unheralded decision of the Thatcher Government to surrender Hong Kong to China without compensation came as a complete surprise. The sole condition that Hong Kong be run on the Chinese 'one country, two systems' principle, with the status of a separate administrative region (SAR), seemed no more than a 'fig leaf' of democracy.

In his memoirs, Sir Percy Craddock, former Governor of Hong Kong, relates how he advised Lady Thatcher and her Foreign Secretary Geoffrey Howe (now Lord Howe) at the time when they were planning to capitulate that Mr Deng as China's 'paramount leader' and its government were ready for a quite different outcome. Although China was entitled unequivocally in international law to the return of Hong Kong Island and the New Territories on the expiry of their leases, it expected Britain to bargain for benefits in return and would have been open to a solution along the lines of permanent shared responsibility for the government and economy of Hong Kong. Sadly, Sir Percy's successor, who had never achieved a comparable relationship with the Chinese leadership, gave contrary advice and his view prevailed.

There is corroboration for Sir Percy Craddock's reading of these expectations. In informal discussions with me and other colleagues, the Senior Municipal People's Government officials in Tianjin, notably Vice Mayor Zhang Zhao Ruo, with whom we were working closely on the London Docklands project, were clear on what they had expected:

'Why could Hong Kong not become an investment joint venture between the governments of China and the UK,' they asked, 'to the mutual economic benefit of both parties?'

For China, whose economic renaissance was spearheaded by foreign-invested JVs, this would have been an entirely logical and acceptable strategy. A similar JV outcome was anticipated by Premier Zhao Ziyang, the former Mayor of Shanghai, in his conversations with us.

Even after the British surrender, we were told, the Chinese Government were prepared to be generous and planned to offer commercial concessions in Hong Kong to the UK. However, the residual goodwill was squandered by Chris Patten when he was appointed the last Governor of Hong Kong by John Major as a consolation prize for losing his seat in the 1984 British General Election. Ridiculed as 'Fat Pang' by Beijing, he adopted an unremitting adversarial stance towards the Chinese leadership in the futile pursuit of trying to embed democratic institutions into Hong Kong prior to the handover, instead of focusing on the harvesting of maximum economic benefits to Hong Kong and Britain. In reality, the political game was lost and won before his appointment as Governor.

Perhaps the last word in this whole sorry saga should go to Prince Charles, who aptly described the actual handover ceremony in 1997 that he attended as 'The Great Chinese Takeaway'.

★

More than 20 years on from these events, the business environment is very different. However, it is equally difficult for would-be paper millionaires to exploit niche opportunities in China. Today, privately owned companies and co-operatives where local towns or village communities are the shareholders account for more than 75 per cent of China's rocketing GDP. The old generation of uneducated bureaucrats who were placed in senior management positions during the Cultural Revolution has thankfully passed on. China's new generation of business executives are young, well educated, often with academic qualifications or business experience from the West and highly motivated. In any JV discussion today it is common for the Chinese senior management to ask for incentive remuneration and stock options, both acceptable to the authorities except in the most hidebound of state-owned enterprises, where the dead hand of bureaucracy still holds sway.

There is also a completely new breed of well-educated Chinese entrepreneurs who have built their own businesses from nothing, often in IT and related fields. They have achieved paper millionaire status by floating their companies' shares on the Hong Kong or one of the two mainland stock exchanges.

In terms of regulation, life has become easier. JVs involving investment up to US$100 million are approved at local branches of the Ministry of Commerce (MOFCOM). Previously, approval for all JVs was required at central government level in Beijing.

Another important change is that Western investors are now allowed to take majority stakes in JVs in most industries, excluding certain protected sectors such as banking, IT, publishing or the media where equity JVs are banned altogether. They may also set up their own businesses using advanced technology or by exporting more than 50 per cent of their products under the umbrella of the Joint Venture Law in a special category of wholly foreign-owned entities (WFOEs). This avoids problems of partner selection but investors still need reliable help to manage approvals and permits from the local authorities.

These are marked improvements but old difficulties remain for those trying to start up in China. The toughest problem is how to identify potential Chinese partners, having decided in what field of activity and in which city or province to do business. The first selection isn't easy either, given the size of the market and the number and variety of thriving business locations.

The conventional routes of using business agencies such as the China Britain Business Council, meeting Chinese companies in visiting trade missions or taking part in a trade mission to China are seldom satisfactory and, unless you are very lucky, will not help you to find a good partner. Typically, Chinese state and local authorities, responding to requests for help or on outward or inward trade missions, trot out those companies most in need of investment, technical or management input and not the brightest or best. Attending trade exhibitions in China may be more successful but the process is still one of searching for needles in a haystack.

Even if you are fortunate in finding a dynamic partner with entrepreneurial, young management, there is still the risk of what is known as 'the mother-in-law' effect. However bright and enthusiastic your prospective partner company may be, its ability to deliver will be affected by the organization to which it reports – the parent company in the case of state-owned enterprises or the local government bureau which supervises its activities. If either of these belongs to the old bureaucratic school, your JV will be dampened and very likely ruined by the dead hand of the mother-in-law's authority. There is no way of determining whether the reporting organization is positive or negative without local knowledge. This was certainly one of the problems I encountered in my early days in China.

The only effective ways of selecting good partners are those described in the first part of this chapter – but 'with Chinese characteristics', as they say when describing China as a market economy.

Squaring the circle

Overall, Chinese businesspeople have done an excellent job in understanding and adapting to the Western mindset – a much better job than we have in understanding theirs. This is a pity because we should not be deceived into thinking that they have abandoned theirs; to succeed in China, the paper millionaire needs to take account of Chinese business culture and protocols.

Personal relationships and personal connections are all-important in China. They permeate family and social life and are more critical to business success than probably any other country. The Chinese system of social interaction is encompassed in the definition of *guanxi*. Whole books and many academic papers have been written about *guanxi* and its relationship to Western networking practices. You don't need to read them to understand how *guanxi* works in Chinese business.

Some people mistakenly believe that *guanxi* is akin to the 'old boy network', whose influence is now somewhat diminished in British business. However, the old boy network is largely a negative influence. As I found to my cost, it is all too often a tool for the 'Establishment' to exclude from of its business those who are not of its number. *Guanxi* has more in common with the alumni associations of American Ivy League universities but its tacit rules of behaviour and obligations are more demanding.

Explained simply, family connections and, more pervasively, friendships acquired at school and university provide the network for educated Chinese in business and in government. The individual may be a member of more than one network and can bring together friends from each so that his personal network becomes extended. These networks provide an invaluable route to those in authority and are only accessible to Westerners through established friendships with network members who will perform introductions within their circle as a personal favour.

The rules of engagement for those within each circle, at the heart of *guanxi,* are very simple. If your friend asks you for help you are bound to do your best to deliver; it may be an introduction, help in securing a university place for a relative or finding employment in the West for a close friend. 'I can't help you' is never an acceptable response. You have to try. It doesn't matter if you fail, so long as it can be seen that you made the effort. The same applies in reverse; your Chinese friend also has to do his best. Only if the first to make a request responds is the return favour obligatory. The same rule also applies to Westerners. Should you give a negative response, you will be excluded and cut off from your friend's circle. Conversely, if you respond positively you are entitled to ask for another favour. Repeated exchanges deepen and strengthen the friendship and open up acceptance by other members of the network.

These personal friendships and access to *guanxi* networks can be cultivated only by living in China or visiting regularly for extended periods over a number of years. 'Old friend' status which is conferred on visitors after one or two meetings only is not at all the same thing and is little more than social recognition of a regular acquaintance.

INDIA

The economic outlook

At first sight the economic prospects and business opportunities appear similar to China. GDP growth is running at above 8 per cent, compared to China's 9.5 per cent plus and similar to that of tiny Latvia, the fastest growing of the new EU members. Gradual economic liberalization since the early 1990s has generated durable growth in previously protected industries. There are a host of dynamic local companies that are competing effectively in international markets in steel, pharmaceuticals and textiles, IT outsourcing and other service sectors. India also has the advantage of domestic market potential, stimulated by a burgeoning middle class, which was slower to develop in China.

However, econometrics can be misleading. Behind the head-lines, GNP per head is only US$2,880 compared to China's US$4,980 and an average US$4,300 for emerging countries. There are only 46 telephones and 7 computers per 1,000 inhabitants, compared with 209 and 27 in China, reflecting the greater poverty and lower proportion of urban inhabitants in India. Given that the impressive growth of the Indian economy is from a low base, the question is whether the growth rate can be sustained and India will follow a similar path to prosperity and domination of specific manufacturing industries.

There are grounds for doubt. India's public sector finances are weak and the debt burden is too heavy to be sustained indefi-nitely. There are major infrastructure deficiencies and the frag-mented composition of the government coalition makes it difficult to introduce structural reforms or address these and other prob-lems. India is admired as the world's largest democracy, but in terms of managing change and stimulating the long-term growth of such an enormous emerging market, democracy may well be a handicap. One prime reason why China has been so successful is that since 1979, it has benefited from a largely benevolent totali-tarian government. This government has been able to deploy macro-economic solutions to many of its problems such as infra-structure and, more recently, the encouragement of private indus-try and reform of the banking system.

Twenty years ago, I predicted with certainty what has happened in China and the boundless opportunities for entrepreneurs. I'm sure that I can do the same for India today. That said, there are glittering opportunities for paper millionaires in the major Indian cities, such as New Delhi, Mumbai or Bangalore, and selected industry sectors today. Certainly, in my field there is little compe-tition and a serious player could achieve in this much larger market four times that which we accomplished in Russia.

The business environment

The difficulties of building business in India are largely because nothing is quite what it seems. On first acquaintance, visitors to India are struck by its colour and beauty, the charm and friendliness of its people and their pro-British attitudes. The business environment appears safe and familiar. But these first impressions are deceptive and disguise endemic risk factors that can make successful business impossible.

At the heart of the problem is the difference between Indian and Western mindsets that is often obscured by the commonality of the language. It is unwise to believe that the correct use of precise English by Indian counterparts implies that they are coming at any issue in the same way as you are or that their perception of what a situation demands is the same as yours. Anyone who has tried to pursue a complaint or correct a misunderstanding with a service supplier's Indian call centre will probably understand what I mean.

For example, as a result of its Imperial heritage, the Indian legal system was adopted from the British system and, in theory, should operate in the same way. When it comes to civil litigation, the Indian judiciary system functions formally as it should but stops short at practical enforcement. Winning a judgment in court may be only the first battle in a prolonged war of attrition. There are countless delaying tactics and legal manoeuvres that can be deployed to challenge court judgements and arbitration awards and to frustrate the execution of justice. The process is dauntingly expensive too with every appeal, further discovery of particulars and registration of documents requiring the payment of substantial fees by the Plaintiff to lawyers, into court or even to ministries. The case study that follows is an example of what can happen.

Just as serious are the unwritten 'grey' rules that can sabotage the trade and investment ventures of any foreign company. The most pernicious of these was the rule that you had to appoint an

Indian national as your agent in India and that the first company with which you did business had the right to be your partner or intermediary in subsequent transactions of whatever nature. For Western companies making a first visit to India and signing a contract to export goods there was a further hazard. Having shipped the goods, payment could be blocked on the basis that the vendor had no appointed agent in India.

Recently, India has formally outlawed the practice of pre-emptive partnership but the legislation is not retrospective and thousands of foreign companies already doing business in India are saddled with exclusive partners that are not to their taste.

CASE STUDY: A DENIAL OF JUSTICE

Eight years ago, two British investors lent a seven-figure sum to an Indian company owned by two local shareholders. The loan was secured by mortgage on the Indian company's property to provide funds for development. Subsequently, the investors and the two Indian shareholders agreed that the loan should be converted into new shares in the company on release of the mortgage charge. A formal agreement to that effect was signed between the British partners and the Indian company.

Under the terms of the agreement, the charge on the company's assets was released and the shares were to be issued by the company as soon as possible but not later than two weeks. Subsequently, the British investors complained of not receiving their shares, although minutes of the company were also produced, approving the transaction on signature of the agreement.

The Indian shareholder argued that the agreement was invalid. He also refused to repay the loan and restore the charge on the company's property. The British partners took the Indian partner and the company to an Indian court. Attempts to enforce a judgement were skilfully frustrated by the Indian partner who took the proceedings to a succession of local courts where by means of

bribes he secured deferment. On each occasion, the British partners were left to pay the legal costs of the court on both sides in
India and London and both sides' solicitors.

In one bizarre ploy, the Indian partner produced a letter on official Ministry letterhead, stating that the British partners should
cease or desist from working or making investments in India as
they had not obtained the Indian partner's permission. He also
had the letter published in the Indian national newspapers. More
lawyers' costs and payments to the various intermediaries over
months were incurred to produce a Ministry denial that the letter
was not genuine.

In a final effort to settle the matter, the British partners invoked
the arbitration clause in the agreement. Although the Indian
partner claimed the agreement was invalid, he agreed to arbitration in London where the British partners were required to pay
US$280,000 to the ICC Court of Arbitration as an advance of the
defendants' and claimants' costs and against an unfavourable
judgement.

After 10 months of hearings in 2006, the court found in favour
of the British investors but the Indian partner claimed that the
court had no jurisdiction over transactions in India.

The partners are pursuing the Indian partners in the Indian
courts but these proceedings are likely to take at least three to
four years. Meanwhile, legal costs have accumulated to over
US$1,000,000 for the British investors compared to US$50,000
for the Indian partner who continues to enjoy his illegal status in
the company as if nothing has happened.

In the light of this experience, I would warn foreign business
people embarking on a venture in India to take extreme care. The
selection of an honest and reliable local partner is a key issue in
any emerging market. In India, it is absolutely critical. The business culture and shortcomings in administration of the law allow
unscrupulous Indian partners to exploit their position to the
maximum by extracting additional payments, defrauding their
Western partners and delaying settlements indefinitely. What is

more, an association with one bad partner in India can preclude you from a further venture in any other field with a new partner.

My conclusions on India are that if you follow the guidelines below you may have a good chance to succeed.

1. Take the trouble to do extra homework by selecting partners who have had other foreign dealings and associations, which you could check out. Also, the more assets the prospective Indian partner may have abroad, the better for you.

2. No matter how attractive your investment opportunity is, take your time to investigate the basis of your investment, permissions and legal requirements, and ensure that all is in order at the time of completion. All payments and investments should be made in escrow until the paperwork is complete, permissions have been granted and actual share certificates are issued.

3. All agreements and or JVs should have a simple termination clause to the agreement and not rely on an arbitration clause. If you are unable to agree such a simple clause, then my advice would be to limit the agreement into time phases. For example, the agreement could be for 25–50 years, with a get-out clause for either party every three years, subject to mutual written agreement of the parties to continue. In that manner, if either party is unhappy with the other, he is free after certain trial periods, with his rights restored.

4. Do not do any favours for any partners or members of your prospective partner's family, no matter how much you like the person. For example, many companies that need to expedite visas are asked to write letters of invitation saying that it is responsible for all expenses as a matter of form in order to obtain them. In case of discord with your partner under these

circumstances, do not be surprised to receive an unexpected bill for expenses and compensation.

5. In all agreements, a clause should be inserted that clearly states that either party is free to operate in India except for the subject matter of the original agreement that has to be narrowly defined to avoid ambiguity and misunderstandings.

6. Never write letters of recommendation for any member of your partner's family to allow entry or employment in your country. In case of disputes, these letters will be used against you in the Indian courts.

7. On all loans or investments in India, it is recommended that you form a special company or subsidiary for this transaction only. Your local company would then borrow the funds from one of the big international banks in India, with a guarantee that you will provide from your bank in your country rather than transferring the funds directly from outside India. The cost of the guarantee is minimal compared to the risks to which you will be otherwise exposed. Also the conditions that the local bank will require from you could alert you to ensure that your lawyers have adequately covered your exposure in the agreement.

8. Last but not least, no matter how friendly your relationship, your private life should not be a subject for discussion.

There is no antidote to stupidity and my final conclusion on India is that if you are unlucky enough to select or acquire a bad or dishonest partner through poor judgement, do not be tempted to engage in litigation to recover your investment, rights or trading loss. Simply write off your investment and walk away.

However, the other side of the coin is the risk/reward ratio. Where else, aside from China and Russia 10 years ago, could you become a key player in a 1.3-billion population market where unexploited opportunities exist in the thousands? Join the multitude of expatriates who have returned to India with little or no capital but the patience to accept a lower standard of living for a few years in order to gain a fortune, before returning in triumph to the world stage.